ADVANCED RAISED BED GARDENING GUIDE

EXPERT TIPS TO OPTIMIZE YOUR YIELD, GROW HEALTHY PLANTS AND TAKE YOUR RAISED BED GARDEN TO THE NEXT LEVEL

PETER SHEPPERD

CONTENTS

THIS CHECKLIST INCLUDES:

- 10 items you will need to maintain your green fingered adventure.
- The highest quality Gardening items.
- Where you can buy these items for the lowest price.

The last thing we want is for your gardening project start to be delayed because you weren't as prepared as you could be.

To receive your essential tool checklist, scan the QR code with your mobile phone camera:

INTRODUCTION

"Gardens are not made by singing 'Oh, how beautiful,' and sitting in the shade."

— RUDYARD KIPLING

This is the second in a series of books designed to help guide the reader along the gently winding path from novice to competent gardener. The first book called "Introduction to Raised bed Gardening" was a bit of a cheat. Not that the information it contained was not pertinent or achievable, but precisely for the opposite reason. I knew that once you had discovered the pleasures of growing your first few plants and vegetables, it was doubtful that you would not want to expand on that knowledge. Gardening is like that. You cautiously dip your toes in the water, and the next thing you know you want to tear your clothes off and swim naked through the vast sea of information the subject has to offer.

This book is designed to build on your existing skillset but never at a pace that becomes too academic or difficult to understand. I don't believe that gardening should ever become so complicated that it falls outside the ordinary person's reach. It has, after all, been practised for thousands of years by very ordinary people, and I don't see why it should now become the preserve of a handful of so-called experts. I have been gardening successfully for more than a decade, and all of my experience was gained from trial, error and the helpful guidance shared with me by those who had travelled the path longer than I had.

Gardeners, you will discover, are a funny breed. It is one of the few occupations where those who practice it are not only happy to share their knowledge, their time and their seeds and cuttings but also seem to delight in doing so. Perhaps it is because they recognise just how generous nature has been to them or perhaps it is just the simple and slow pace of life that nature dictates that makes them this way. I now try to share some of that wealth of information with you, confident in the knowledge that you too will pass it on somewhere down the line.

In this book, I will be sharing ways to expand your raised bed gardening to a different level. We will explore design in a little more depth as well as considering a far more comprehensive range of plants to grow. Whether your ambitions are just to augment your homegrown supplies or to dive right in and try to grow all of the vegetables you and your family consume, at the end of this book you will have all the knowledge you need to achieve your goals.

Figure 1. Grow more food in less space.

Hopefully, the first book in this series has already demonstrated just how productive this type of gardening can be and what a fantastic yield you can achieve in a relatively small space. Now we will consider ways to expand on that yield and also to bring in a whole range of more advanced crops that you might once have considered too difficult to grow yourself. You should have overcome that initial lack of confidence by now and be eager to build on that foundation that the first book laid for you.

Figure 2. Extend your growing season with winter crops.

Another aspect we will be looking at will be expanding your season so that you can reap the benefits of winter crops that are so often ignored by the small-scale gardener. These provide a vital harvest at a time when so many gardens lie idle or only support a cover crop. All of this new information I will endeavour to convey in the same simple terminology that I hope dominates this entire series. I want this to be a gradual and enjoyable learning experience rather than an attempt to overcomplicate what should not be an overly complicated subject. Gardening, at the end of the day, should be a pleasure. One that helps sustain you and your family and the environment at the same time.

1

LAYOUTS

At this stage, I am working on the assumption that the reader has read the "Introduction to Raised Bed gardening" book or has had a season or two of gardening under his or her belt using the raised bed method. The fact that you have chosen to push on and expand your knowledge demonstrates that you have found that the method works and hopefully have become as enthusiast about raised beds as I am. It is a very practical method, and if it would only cause me to lose weight or stop losing hair, it would, in my opinion, be perfect.

Now it is time to move forward and turn your garden into something of a small farm. The temptation at this stage is to just cram in as many raised beds as possible and get growing, but I would urge a little patience here.

Now that the whole concept is no longer new, you can start to consider not only the practicalities but also the design features that you most value. We have looked at some of the materials that beds can be made of in the last book. In this book, we are going to look at some more of these and also at some more daring designs. As always, good design starts on paper before it is put onto the ground.

Figure 3. Growing vegetables in deep raised beds.

The thing you must grasp is that you are not limited just to boxes and right rectangles. I always believe that even the most functional of gardens can include some design elements that will add to the aesthetic appeal. There is no reason why a raised bed garden should not be both pleasing to the eye and functional at the same time. When you first start with this method, it is new and, as with most things in life, it is best to keep things simple. Now is the time to be more daring and the best place to do that is on a piece of paper.

Firstly, you need to look at your existing beds and decide what worked and what didn't. Were your beds placed where they would catch that ideal six to eight hours a day of sunlight? Could you have made access more simple and was water readily available? If these crucial criteria were all met, then you will probably want to continue to garden where you do at the moment. If not, then now is the time to search for a more suitable environment. If the existing garden is perfectly placed, you will need to consider whether you simply want to add on to what you have already or start from scratch. It may seem like a waste of time pulling existing beds apart and rebuilding, but in reality, a few days of extra work will fade into oblivion once you have created the garden of your dreams. Be daring and dream big is my advice. You will also have learned a great deal about the materials you built with the first time around, and you might believe that it is time for a change.

What I want you to grasp is that beds can be of any shape that you care to build them. You need to consider ease of access from all sides, but you know that already, so are well placed on incorporating that into your new design. I have known gardeners to become so enthralled with the raised bed concept that they converted their whole garden to this format. All beds were raised but by the innovative use of both height and shape, and they were able to produce something breathtakingly beautiful both for their vegetable garden and for their flower garden.

Figure 4. Advanced gardening goals.

Once you have decided beyond doubt where the raised bed garden is to be, you will need to measure it out and draw it to scale. In the first book, where simple shapes were used, you were able to do a reasonably rough measurement. Now you will need to be more accurate and you will probably need to use a long tape measure and some fixed points to be sure that what you have on paper corresponds to what you will have on the ground. We will deal with this part of the design process in much more depth in the book on Urban Gardening, which is part of this series.

In order to measure accurately, you are going to use a system called triangulation. This requires you to measure from two set points to create a triangle, thus ensuring that the point you are measuring to remains fixed. For example, if a point is five meters from a fence, it is very difficult when putting it on paper, to know where on the drawing it should go. If on the other hand, that same point is ten meters from one end of the fence and nine meters from the other end of the fence, that position becomes fixed. This means that as long as you have taken your measurements correctly, the position you have marked can only be in the position where the nine and ten-meter marks intersect.

It will take a while to get the plan laid out on paper but take your time over this part of the operation because it is crucial. It is the accuracy you produce now that enables you to reproduce your design from paperback onto the ground at a later stage. I would recommend that you draw out the garden on graph paper after deciding what scale fits the paper most appropriately. At the end of the measuring out process, you should have an accurate and to scale plan of the outline of the garden, including any features like sheds or trees. You should also have an accurate mark as to where taps and water sources are and where north is. Once you are sure that the plan is a to-scale representation of what is on the ground then make several photocopies. Pour a large cup of tea (red wine will do as a substitute) and let your imagination go wild.Certain practicalities will always remain important. Your paths will need to be wide enough to accommodate a wheelbarrow comfortably, you will need to be able to access the plants easily without having to walk

Figure 5. Planning is crucial when designing your dream garden.

on the beds, and you will need to consider where the sun will fall. Other than that, you can be as creative as you want to be. I have seen star-shaped beds, U shaped beds and round beds. Even a spiral can be made using packed rocks. This gives you a spiral that gradually mounts at the centre in a shape reminiscent of a snail's shell and makes for a beautiful eye-catching focal point.

Figure 6. A pyramid bed used to maximise the strawberry harvest.

Always be on the lookout for inspiration, and you will be surprised where you find it. Landscape architects designed many of those desiccated looking beds you see in shopping centre car parks. Beneath the sad looking plants there is often a creative structural plan, and there may be ideas there that help you develop the skeleton for your garden. Garden magazines and the internet are teeming with design ideas, and by now you are probably already addicted to some of the many gardening shows on television. What you will need to do is sit down with the photocopied plans of the garden skeleton and draw out different options until you come up with a design that pleases you. Don't expect this to be a one attempt and all is done process. It requires numerous re-workings and even the most experienced of garden designers draws and redraws before he gets a result that he is ultimately happy with. That is why I suggested taking several photocopies of the plan you measured. You can sketch away to your heart's content and then start a new plan if you don't achieve a pleasing enough result.

The drawing may be two dimensional, but that doesn't mean the garden needs to be. Think about beds of differing heights as well as arbours between beds or trellises up which climbers and vines can scramble. If you have the room, then throw in a water feature or a couple of nice outdoor sculptures. It doesn't matter if you don't have any or can't afford them right now. If they are built into the plan, they can always be added at a later stage.

At the end of any design process, my kitchen floor is covered with balls of paper that bare testimony to early failed drawings. Hopefully, however, somewhere on the table is a pristine design that perfectly adheres to both my desires and the practicalities of the garden I want. Each of those failures on the floor added a little something to what turned out to be the end result. For many of my gardening acquaintances and me, the design process is one of the more creative parts of gardening so wallow in it rather than shy away from it.

In my use of the pen and paper approach, I am something of a dinosaur. Today there is a myriad of garden design computer programs that eliminate the need for piles of paper and go a little way toward saving the planet at the same time. Unfortunately, as far as my abilities are concerned, the planet will have to suffer a little longer because I simply lack the computer design skills. Those that have patiently tried to train me in that direction have all eventually had to accept that I have the computer abilities of a somewhat dim-witted King Charles spaniel.

Whatever route you choose to follow in the design process, always have practicality in the back of your mind. Some materials lend themselves freely to curves and bends while others don't. I like to decide well in advance what material the beds will be made of and then design accordingly, rather than the other way around. Knowing what materials you will be using often determines what bed shapes can be built. If I am working with wooden beds, for example, it is not possible to make one in the form of a circle. We looked at several materials in the first book on raised beds, but you might want to skip ahead to the next chapter to look at some slightly different options before you make a final decision.

We looked at several materials in the first book on raised beds and discussed the best types of wood and specifically Cedar wood. We also looked at railway sleepers, plastic planks, pre-made kits and willow and/or wattle, but you might want to skip ahead to the next chapter to look at some slightly different options before you make a final decision.

It is also wise to know beforehand what your paths are to be made from. If you are just throwing down bark or wood chips, then it won't be a problem, but if you want a more rigid material such as brushed concrete, then you must consider when this will be poured during the build process. Be realistic about your ability to build the garden you design if you are planning on doing the work yourself. There are few things more frustrating than having the perfect design on paper but then finding you lack the ability to convert those plans to reality. You can, of course, hire the services of a profes-sional but please speak to them in advance so that they can have some input as to what is practically possible and what can only be done with the backup of a team from NASA.

I am hoping that all that you have read in this book so far points clearly to one thing. Thinking things out in advance is critical. The more complex your design, the more difficult the build and the more accurate you will need to be when laying the plan out on the ground. You will need to find that elusive balance between great design and functionality. On the one hand, I am trying to encourage you to be daring, and on the other, I probably seem like I am holding you back by reminding you of the restrictions imposed by practicality. Somewhere between those two parameters, there is a solution and if you take your time, seek outside inspiration and are creative, you will find it. I find it helps to remind myself that I am working with natural materials and that by combining those with a well thought out design, I can't go too far wrong. Most of the ugly things we see in this world do not incorporate natural materials very much.

So far, we have been looking at this whole design process from the point of view of fixed beds. There is the option, however, of making beds that are movable and with raised beds, this is entirely feasible. There are a few reasons for a gardener to choose to go down this route. The most common is where only a small area is available, and it becomes necessary to move the beds during the day to access the maximum amount of light. This is often the case on apartment patios. As the light moves, part of the patio may become shaded by the building or neighbouring buildings. By only moving the beds from one side of the patio to the other, this lack of light issue might be overcome. Another instance might be where there is only a little amount of space on a terrace or deck. The raised beds can be placed and planted but should the space be needed as an entertainment area occasionally; the beds could be temporarily moved out of the way.

Figure 7. Wooden crates are perfect mobile beds.

There is any number of easy ways to make mobile beds. They can be made from plastic milk crates with some lining to retain the soil, or they can be purpose-built. Something of a similar shape to a table but with raised sides to hold soil and some drainage holes would make a fine bed to grow a few herbs or some of the smaller vegetables such as carrots and radishes. If it were to have wheels, then moving it from one place to another would become that much easier.

We looked quite extensively at building raised beds in the first book on the subject. In the next chapter, we will look at some slightly less common options.

2

UNORTHODOX RAISED BED MATERIALS

Once you have drawn out your plan, you now need to reproduce that drawing on the ground. This requires you to reverse the process with as much accuracy as possible. You will need to take out your extra-long tape measure again and using the same fixed points as you did for the plan you will now need to mark your beds out on the ground upon which the garden is to be built. You can lay them out using pegs and sticks, but I suggest you pop into your local builders' merchant and purchase a can of marking out spray. Laying out the bed with strings and canes almost always leads to problems as they move so easily.

With the corners of each bed marked out from the drawing, it is a relatively simple matter to join up the dots using the spray and a straight edge if you don't think you can manage free hand. Once your beds are drawn out on the ground, you will start to get a far better feel for what the finished garden is going to look like. If possible, try to get a bit of a birds-eye view by looking down on the beds from a first-floor window or even a step ladder. This will be your final opportunity to make sure that what you have marked out corresponds precisely with your scale plan.

Wooden frames have traditionally dominated raised beds. There are many different options and here are some that we have not looked at in as much depth as we did the wooden beds in book one. Each comes with advantages and disadvantages which you will need to consider in terms of your particular circumstances, building capabilities and budget.

Cement blocks are sturdy, long-lasting and allow you the opportunity to make beds of almost any shape. Laying blocks is quite physically demanding, but if you can handle the physical exercise, they are not that difficult to lay. You will need to run a small concrete foundation and then lay the blocks using sand and cement. This may seem a little bit like the work of an expert bricklayer, but it is relatively easy though the blocks are heavy. As long as you can mix a four to one sharp sand to cement mix and use a spirit level, then laying blocks is not beyond the reach of any home handyman.

Another factor that might help you be a little more confident is that you are unlikely to need to go more than two courses high. If you were to set about making a building with no experience, then I might be a little less quick to encourage you to give it a go yourself.

Figure 8. Concrete raised beds are a wonderful addition for a more contemporary feel.

Blocks come in differing widths and you want the wider ones which are six inches wide. They are heavier but they will give you excellent beds that will last for many years. For a more superior appearance, you can plaster the outsides with a waterproof plaster and finish off the tops with wood or tiles. I come from an area rich in limestone, and once I have built my beds, I clad them in flat pieces of stone which makes the beds look like they are made from stone but at a fraction of the price. To attach the stone to the blocks, you mix some lime powder with sand and cement, and they stick quite easily.

A totally different effect can be had by building beds from straw bales. This is one of the easiest materials to use as you just lay the bales end to end and you have a deep bed in which to lay your planting medium. They are cheap, usually quite readily available and the whole garden can be built in virtually no time. If you want to put up plant

Figure 9. Ready to lay straw bales.

supports or trellis, the posts can just be stabbed into the bales themselves. There is nothing new about this system, and it has been used for hundreds of years in various places throughout the world.

It is essential to understand the difference between straw and hay. Straw is made from the leftover stems of crops such as wheat, barley or alfalfa. Hay is made from dried cut grass. Hay will break down much more quickly than straw, but more importantly, it has not had the heads cut off before being baled, and so contains seeds. Not only will there be grass seeds but it will also contain the seeds of any weeds that will have grown in the grass. I am not saying don't use hay; you need to be aware that it does not come with the same benefits of straw, and you will have a weed problem.

Beds built from straw bales will generally last only one season if you live in a hot and wet area, two at the most. As the straw breaks down, it adds other nutrients to your beds which is a plus. When you are done with the bales, it makes a good winter mulch or can be mixed with manure to rot down into great compost slowly. New beds can then be built using the same method. Straw is porous meaning that beds will drain quite quickly though I find the bales tend to absorb excess water which helps keeps the whole bed moist.

If you feel that this is a good route for you then make sure that you layout your beds on a dry day. Moving wet straw bales is a lot more physically demanding than moving dry ones. Another advantage that straw bales have is that you get to change your garden design every year or two. When the time comes to exchange the old bales for new ones you might like to shake things up a bit and go for a whole garden makeover which few other raised bed materials offer.

Galvanised metal is one of my favourite choices when building raised beds. At first, the idea sounds more practical than attractive, but I frame the individual sheets with pieces of two by four timber. This makes them easy to bolt together while at the same time making the beds far more attractive and less utilitarian looking than if I were to simply hold the sheets up with stakes. It makes them more secure, and a dark stain on the wooden frames contrasts nicely with the clean look of the metal. It is easy enough to cut the sheets with an angle grinder so I can get a variety of bed shapes, but I cannot make curved forms using this material. Some companies supply pre-made galvanised beds which just need to be bolted together. These come with preformed rounded ends which is quite pleasing to the eye. They also offer a choice of coloured powder coat finishes so you aren't restricted to just that shiny galvanised effect.

If you live in an agricultural area, you can sometimes purchase galvanised feed troughs from agricultural suppliers. These tend to be round with a four-foot diameter and three feet high. If you want round beds, then this may be an easy route to go down. Just have some feed troughs delivered, drill plenty of drainage holes in the bottom and fill with growing medium, and you are good to go.

Galvanised beds come with many advantages, but there are some drawbacks you might need to consider. They do get hotter than wooden beds and you may need to water slightly more often.

Figure 10. Circular galvanised beds make excellent gardening containers.

They also don't drain so you will need to ensure that the ground beneath these beds is free draining or your beds will become a swamp. That said, I still believe that they provide a very practical, long-lasting and attractive option.

Some people have taken to building the walls of their beds from old car tires, and this has caused something of a controversy in the gardening world. Tires are free, readily available and easy to build with. They can also be laid in a wide array of shapes. The controversy arises over the fact that they are made from petroleum-based materials. Whilst nobody has done tests as to whether or not these will leach into the soil and cause toxicity, the possibility does exist.

What I believe is that even if the tires do break down, they are not going to do so in a hurry. It should, therefore, be relatively safe if you only use them for a year or two and then replace them. I should also point out that I have absolutely no scientific evidence for this theory and that you should therefore not regard it as of any value whatsoever. I have, however, been growing potatoes in tires for years and so far have suffered no noticeable ill effects other than a slight thickening of the waist. This could equally be attributed to red wine consumption which does take place from time to time.

There is one other option for raised beds that is not so much a material option as a change in methodology. This method, known as the hotbed method, has been used since Victorian times to grow plants during the colder months. The bottom three-quarters of the bed is filled with manure while the top quarter is then filled with your choice of growing medium. As the manure breaks down, it rapidly increases the temperature of the soil, and this gives you a longer growing season and enables you to grow plants such as pineapples which you would not usually be able to grow unless you lived closer to the equator.

Victorian gardeners were famed for the ability to put unusual food on the tables of their wealthy employers at times when things like pineapple would only have been an expensive imported luxury. The hotbed was one of their favourite methods for doing this, and most Victorian glasshouses had a raised bed built into them. The beds tended to be built from brick and were usually about two feet high. If you want to experiment with this system, you could do so as long as your raised bed were at least eighteen inches high. It works both indoors and outdoors but the extra heat lasts only for about two months at which point the beds need to be emptied and refilled.

Whatever material you decide on, remember that the plants don't care, what your raised bed is doing as acting as a container for an ideal growing medium. The choice you make, therefore depends on your budget, your building ability and what sort of look you want to achieve. If you start by looking through reclaimed material yards and things like Craigslist and the internet, you may well find bargains that influence your choice of material.

One of the most impressive raised bed gardens that I have seen was made from a series of old bathtubs laid end to end down a hill. Watering was done by filling the top bath bed which was connected to the next one via a pipe from the plug hole to the overflow hole. Gradually by just adding water to the top bed, it would flow down to the lowest bed, and the depth of the baths was perfect for raised beds. I am not suggesting that you rush out and buy up every old bath you can get your hands on. I am only offering this as an example of what a little out of the box thinking can produce, and to show just what a versatile system the raised bed garden can provide.

3

EXPERIMENTING WITH VARIOUS PLANT GROWING TECHNOLOGIES

One of the things that many gardeners struggle to come to terms with is that gardening is as much art as it is science. Because we live in a world where so much is human-made and is defined by rigidly fixed criteria, it is easy to assume that a fixed set of rules governs everything we deal with. In gardening, this is very often not the case. Here we are dealing with nature, and many of her rules are more flexible and forgiving than those we choose to impose upon ourselves. It follows, therefore, that there is more than one method of gardening in just about every instance you can think of. Personally, I like the fact that I'm not restricted to just one tightly governed way of doing things. It gives me the freedom to experiment, try different methods and be that little bit more creative than I might have been in another field of work. This is not to suggest that we can simply do what we want to and go against all of the rules that nature does apply, but at the same time, she allows us a level of freedom that we may not be used to.

Figure 11. Loose yourself in the art of gardening.

For some people, this lack of rigidity can be a little disconcerting. Rules offer some people clarity and the security of knowing that they are not going wrong. In this chapter, we are going to be looking at some alternative ways of doing things. They are neither right nor wrong. They merely offer the gardener an alternative approach and very often, as the gardener grows in experience and confidence, he tends to reach a point where he can mix and match different techniques to create something that becomes uniquely his own. Think of it as being like a recipe. The first time you make a new dish you diligently follow the rules, accurately measure out quantities and stick to a strict palette of ingredients. Once you've cooked the dish a couple of times, you quickly reach a point where you can place your mark on it to make it more unique to yourself.

I believe that gardeners and chefs have a great deal in common. The world of cooking would not be the same, and our diets would be a whole lot blander if chefs didn't step out of their comfort zone and push the boundaries. In my opinion, the same thing applies to gardening. It is a field in which each of us has learnt and benefited from the experiments and experience of those who went before us. I wouldn't go so far as to say that I believe it is beholden on us to explore new methods. I do think, though, that experimentation can benefit the whole gardening community. Even if you are one of those people who is happier when governed by rules, I would still encourage you to have a look at these techniques and see if there is not something to be gained from incorporating some of the ideas into your own garden. As ancient as it is, gardening remains a continually evolving process, and mixing and matching is one way in which you can develop your skills as a gardener. As well as stamping your unique way of doing things onto your gardening, you will be pioneering new methods for the gardeners that come after you. The methods that we're about to look at are actually quite old and have been well tested; it is only by adding your own subtle twists to them that you may see something new emerge. I should point out that my theory on experimentation in the garden is not popular with everyone and many gardeners believe that we should stick diligently to the rules. I will leave it to you to decide just how much or how little you want to combine the different techniques. Personally, I am as attracted to the art as I am to the science. With all of my experimenting over the years, I have had my share of failures, but I have always tried to learn from them. The adventures they have provided have helped to keep my passion for gardening as alive today as it was when I first started out.

The first alternative system we're going to look at is straw bale gardening. I know that we have already looked at this material in the context of using the bales as the actual frame of our raised beds. In this instance, we are going to look at them as a means of replacing the planting medium with the straw bales themselves. In other words, we are not going to use them to create our frame; we are going to use them actually to grow our plants. There are several reasons for going down this route. Straw bales can be used as a planting medium on top of any base, including concrete, and they use less labour as there is not any digging or tilling involved. Because they are warmer, they can dramatically extend the growing season both in the spring and in the autumn. They are particularly useful, however, in situations where getting soil or other planting mediums is difficult either because of price, availability or access. Easy to move around, they are cheap and generally tend to be readily available.

Growing on bales offers immediate height, so your physical effort is reduced, they can be used in small spaces, and they require virtually no weeding. Any weeding that is required tends to be very easy because the roots of the weeds are not bound securely into the straw. With this method, you also eliminate the risk of soil-borne diseases. Because they can be used on any type of base, this method is ideal when gardening on concrete surfaces and therefore provides a method for people living in an apartment to grow plants on their terrace. Finally, their rough surface means you will hardly ever have problems from either snails or slugs.

Of course, as with any other type of gardening, this system does come without some drawbacks. Straw bales dry up more quickly, and water control becomes very important. You will also need to fertilise them with some sort of organic fertiliser because this is what will supply the food for your plants, especially in the initial stages.

You can typically purchase straw bales from garden centres, stables or home depots. The best place to get them, however, is directly from the farmer and the best straw is always going to be

Figure 12. Brown hay will require more weeding.

that made with organic material. They can be made from wheat, oats, rye or barley. You can also use linseed or flax if it is available, both of which are slower to break down because of their oil content. There will be occasions when you are unable to get straw bales, and all that you have access to is hay. The difference between hay and straw is that the flowering heads are incorporated into the hay bales. This is quite a crucial point because it means that weeds will become an issue. That said, if you don't mind doing a bit of weeding, the nutrient supply in hay bales is actually far higher than it is in straw bales.

Before you can use straw bales as a growing medium, they first need to be prepared. There are a couple of ways of doing this, but they both amount to the same thing. The objective is to get the bales to a point where they are starting to decompose because it is the decomposing plant material that will provide the food for your new plants. Both methods of doing this will take about two weeks.

Once you have purchased your straw bales, place them in the position where you intend to do your gardening before you start conditioning them. Dry bales are easy to move around, but wet ones become considerably heavier. If you have built raised beds and are using the bales as your growing medium, simply drop your bales into the beds. The next thing you must do is wet the bales down. On the first day, water them thoroughly and then on days two and three water them again on a daily basis. After that, on days four to ten water and feed them with a liquid feed such as compost tea or manure soaked in water until it has dissolved. If you don't fancy making your liquid fertiliser, there are commercial products that you can buy, but you will need to find an organic option.

From the eleventh day to the thirteenth day, you can stop the feeding and just keep the bales damp which will now require less water as they will have started to become saturated. Finally, on the fourteenth day, plunge your hand into the bale to test the heat. The interior should be warm but still slightly cooler than body temperature. This heating process has been brought about by the breaking down of the plant material in a fermentation like process. At its peak, which should have occurred at around day six or seven, the interior of a bale could climb to as high as 65° c (150°F). At that temperature, it would have been far too hot for plants to survive but now as it cools it is in a perfect state for plant growth.

The second method is slightly different, but you are trying to achieve precisely the same result and you should opt for whichever method suits you. On days one, three and five, sprinkle the bales with a generous quantity of dry organic fertiliser and then water in generously. On days two four and six simply soak the bales without adding any feed. On days seven eight and nine, you feed again with one and a half cups of fertiliser per pale per day.

From day eleven, you start watering daily again and by day fourteen, the temperature within the bales should be just below body temperature. As you can see, this is a different route to get to the same place and your method will often be dictated by the choice of fertilisers you have available. It usually takes about two gallons to soak a bale but rather than getting into a complicated water measuring situation, simply apply enough water that it starts to run out the bottom of the bale. As the inside of the bale starts to break down, don't be surprised if you start to see a few mushrooms appearing on the surface. In fact, this is a good sign as it proves that the bacterial action is well underway.

As we have already mentioned, there are no hard and fast rules here. Once you become accustomed to working with the bales, you will start to develop the experience to alter the recipe to suit your personal tastes and conditions.

Figure 13. You can plant directly into your bales using seeds or seedlings.

Finally, after two weeks of conditioning, your bales are at last ready, and you can now plant directly into them. If you are planting seeds, then sprinkle a layer of soilless seed compost so that they have something to get rooted into initially. If you are planting seedlings, then make a hole big enough to accommodate the whole root ball then pop the plant out of its container and plant the whole root ball into the straw. You will follow the same planting distances as you would if you were planting into a soil-based medium.

You can grow just about any plant that you would be able to grow under normal circumstances but be aware that the roots will not gain quite as much support as they would in denser soil. This means that top-heavy plants like corn will need to be staked. Placing stakes and other supports is dead easy because you can just stab them down into the bale. Most of the larger plants that might be prone to tipping can be overcome in smaller dwarf varieties, so this might also be something to consider.

Root crops like carrots and turnips will gradually weaken the bale. This won't be an issue if your bales are contained in a raised bed, but if they are standing in the open it will shorten their longevity.

As I seldom get more than one season from my bales, this does not really alter my planting plan. Potatoes do fine in bales if they are planted at a depth of about six inches. They can be earthed up by just continuing to cover with straw rather than soil. Leave an inch or two of leaf protruding each time. If you want to avoid the earthing up process then just plant them deeper. Sixteen to eighteen inches should give you a generous crop.

Figure 14. Straw used to cover a wooden raised bed.

Whether you are growing from seed or from seedlings, you will need to water in with a fine sprinkler and then water at least once daily. Poke your finger into the bales near your plants from time to time to ensure that the growing medium is always slightly damp. With bales, drying out can occur relatively quickly, and one of the downsides to this method is that you will need to be more attentive than you might need to be in a soil-based medium.

Once a week you will need to feed your plants with a liquid feed. There are dozens of options. You may have been making your own fertiliser tea, but you could also use products such as a blood meal, fish meal or a seaweed-based product. All of these are available at garden centres.

At the end of the growing season, you can examine your bales and decide if they are in good enough condition to use for one more season. In my experience, they seldom are, especially if I have produced a lot of root crops that year. If you are lucky, store the bales somewhere dry until the following spring and then reuse them. If not, mix them into your compost to break down or use them as a mulch on other beds.

Figure 15. Cabbage grown in straw bales.

SQUARE FOOT GARDENING:

Square foot gardening is a concept that has been around since the nineteen-eighties. It was the brainchild of a retired engineer by the name of Mel Bartholomew, and his book Square Foot Gardening has gone on to become a gardening classic. Once Mel retired, he devoted himself to gardening and with an engineer's practical approach to things he was soon finding ways to reduce labour and increase yields. The method he invented is said to enable a gardener to produce the same quantity of crops in twenty per cent of the space.

In America, the concept gained huge momentum and Mel soon become something of a celebrity with a very popular television series that ran for several years. The method is particularly pertinent to people who want to produce vegetables on a small amount of space. As the name implies, beds are divided up into one-foot squares and then each square is planted with a different crop or companion plant. What makes their productivity so high is that no land is lost to paths and the squares are heavily planted so that weeding is kept to a minimum.

If you follow Mel's suggestion, beds will be four foot by four foot thus providing sixteen planting squares. This easily facilitates access from all sides without the need to walk on the bed. If this sounds familiar, it is because the same thinking went into the raised bed system, and the two methods offer plenty of scope to overlap one another. If you have existing raised beds, you can simply divide them up into one-foot squares. To do this, you can nail a latticework of wooden laths to form a trellis of one-foot squares over the bed, or you can mark out the squares with string. How you do this will depend entirely on the material your raised beds are made of and how rigidly you want to stick to the system.

Figure 16. Homegrown garden lettuce in a wooden raised bed.

If you don't have a raised bed already, you can make one out of six to twelve-inch wide planks with lap joints cut out of them every twelve inches. The planks then simply slot into one another, giving you sixteen-foot square beds. At the end of the season, the planks are then just detached and stored for the next season. If you are planning on gardening with children, you might want to drop the bed size down to three foot by three foot. You will only have nine beds, but the children should be able to reach most parts of the bed without needing to walk on the soil or the plants.

Using this method, there is hardly any thinning required and you, therefore, use far less seed. Each square is planted with a predetermined number of plants depending on the crop. See the chart below. Rather than sprinkling a whole row of seed and then thinning, you drop just two or three seeds into the requisite number of planting holes and then just snip off the two weakest seedlings with a scissor once they set their first true leaves.

As with other raised bed systems, it usually is easy to attach a trellis or other support for climbing crops. As we have already seen, these taller plants will need to be planted on the northern end of the bed in the northern hemisphere and the southern end in the southern hemisphere so that they don't cast a shadow over your smaller crops.

Another secret to the square foot gardening method was, of course, the growing mix. Mel's recipe calls for one third peat moss, one-third vermiculite and one-third compost or potting soil. The recipe is still widely used by raised bed gardeners and you will often hear the term Mel's mix or Mel's magic mix in gardening circles. Now at least you will know what people are referring to.

If you are like me and you question the environmental impact of using peat moss, then it can be replaced by coir, potting soil or rice husks. Vermiculite is a mineral that is mined for different purposes, but in gardening terms, it is used for its moisture retention.

Though you will often hear the term Mel's mix, it is far from the only growing medium available to the ardent raised bed gardener, and we will be looking at this subject in more detail further into the book.

Plant	Plants per Square	Plant	Plants per Square
Arugula	4	Okra	1
Basil	4	Onion	4
Bean-Bush	1-4	Parsnips	16
Bean-Pole	1-4	Peas	1
Beets	9	Peppers	1
Brussels Sprouts	1	Pigeon Peas	1
Cabbage	1	Pumpkin	1
Chinese Cabbage	9	Radicchio	2-4
Carrots	16	Radish	16
Corn	4	Rhubarb	1
Cucumber	2	Rutabaga	4
Eggplant	1	Shallots	4
Greens-baby harvest	16	Spinach	9
Greens-mature harvest	4-8	Squash-summer	1
Kale	1	Squash-winter	1
Kohlrabi	4	Sweet Potato	1
Leeks	4-8	Swiss Chard	4
Lettuce-heading	1-4	Tomatillo	1
Lettuce-loose leaf	4	Tomatoes	1
		Turnips	9
Broccoli	1 (18" spacing is best)		
Cauliflower	1 (18" spacing is best)		

Herbs	Herbs per Square	Fruit	Fruit per Square
Basil	4	Garden Huckleberry	1
Calendula	1-4	Melon	1 (18"-24" spacing is best)
Chives	9	Watermelon	1 (18"-24" spacing is best)
Cilantro	9		
Dill	1		
Fennel	4		
Oregano	1		
Parsley	1		
Rosemary	1		
Sage	1		
Tarragon	1		
Thyme	4		

THE NO-DIG METHOD:

This is another gardening method that has quite a long pedigree. It works on the concept that the less you manipulate the soil, the more the microbes and organisms will increase, and the healthier your soil will become. Digging is hard physical work, and although the raised bed method reduces the amount of digging to be done and cuts out much of the bending, many gardeners are happy to avoid it altogether.

No-dig gardening was not devised with the raised bed gardener in mind, but as a way to reduce work when gardening in open ground. Fortunately, this method combines very well with raised bed methodology and you, therefore, have the opportunity to explore the best of both worlds. We will start looking at how it is done in the open ground and then have a look at how to combine the methodology with our raised beds.

The idea is that a garden can be created, even on grass or weeds, without needing to pre-dig the soil. The area to be planted should be covered in a deep layer of compost, and over time, lack of light and air will kill the underlying plants. Often when creating the first bed, the gardener will lay down sheets of cardboard to make it doubly difficult for weeds and grass to survive. The compost will be laid on top of that to a depth of about six inches. A month later, the bed can be planted. Some weeds will make it through the compost, but they will do so in a very weakened state and are therefore extremely easy to deal with. Once the crop is harvested, simply add another two to three inches of compost, firm down lightly, and the bed is ready to be planted again.

When using this method on the ground, there will be places where really aggressive weeds demand firmer action, and in cases like this, a sheet of dark plastic can be laid over the planned bed for a month. After that, the plastic can be rolled back, and a two to three-inch layer of compost spread before replacing the plastic sheet over the bed, complete with its layer of compost.

Figure 17. Perforated gardening film to minimise weeding.

After another month, the bed will be ready for planting. Without even removing the plastic, holes can be simply cut through where the new plants are wanted, and the seedlings can be planted into the layer of compost through the hole.

On some studies done side by side with the traditional dig system, yields are in the region of twenty-five per cent higher with far less physical effort having been brought into play. Furthermore, analysis of the soil has revealed that it remains more tightly bound together which gives it a better structure.

If you have been gardening in raised beds for a while, you will know that much of what you have just read is very similar to the techniques you will already be used to using. Before filling your beds, you may already have been putting down a layer of cardboard to suppress weeds and most of the digging you have been doing has been merely to incorporate new compost or growing medium at the end of each season.

To combine the two methods, the only real difference would be that after harvesting your crops, you would now just top up the bed with two or three inches of healthy compost. Other than firming it down by giving it a few slaps with the back of a shovel, there would be no further preparation to do. Don't worry if the new layer of compost is slightly deeper than the tops of your beds. Compost is continuously breaking down, and it will soon reduce in depth. It is important to firmly tamp it down because plants will not grow as success-fully if the compost is too loose.

Deep digging and double digging are methods that gardeners have been using for centuries, but science is now having its say. What it is telling us is that much of that back-breaking labour could have been avoided. When gardening in open ground on heavy clay soils, there would have been benefits from intense digging. I think that this is where this system somehow became accepted practice. It is still widely taught today at many horticultural and gardening colleges and universities, but it now looks as though the no-dig method will begin to fall from favour.

VERTICAL GARDENING:

Vertical gardening is a method of growing plants in containers suspended from walls. It uses very similar methods to those use in raised beds, and the two systems can be incorporated and will complement each other perfectly.

What vertical gardening does, is that it utilises space that would otherwise have been lost to the gardener. It is very useful if you have a walled garden or even just a bare wall that would provide you somewhere to hang your containers. It is an excellent method for gaining extra capacity where space is at a premium and the apartment patio is the perfect example. What the wall does is provide support for whatever hanging garden system you opt for. You increase your growing area and at the same time, you turn what might have been a bland or even ugly wall into something of abundant beauty. This system really can provide the gardener with some stunning results and can be used for edible crops or ornamental ones or perhaps a combination of the two.

There are many ways of turning walls into growing space, but whichever method you decide to go for, you must ensure that there is no possibility of water ingress. The method is becoming quite popular, and as a result, there are now companies that specialise in kits for this type kind of gardening. If that is out of your budget or you simply prefer to create your own vertical beds, there are other options. These include suspended containers made from horticultural fabric with pocket like planting spaces sown in, wooden or plastic planters on hooks or even plastic bottles suspended in frames.

That might sound a little ugly, but as soon as it is planted up, the foliage transforms the wall into something almost exotic looking. As with all container gardening, watering is something that needs to be taken into consideration, and you will need to feed your plants from time to time with an organic liquid feed.

Figure 18. A plain brick wall turned into a wonderful growing space that also pleases the eye.

There will be more on this subject in the book on container gardening later in this series. Generally, these walls tend to be small enough that they can be watered just with a watering can or a wand attached to a hose. If you are planning on really going for it and covering a lot of wall space, you might want to consider building a drip irrigation system into your construction plan. Some of the premanufactured systems come with an inbuilt method of redirecting excess water from the planters down to the lower ones so that by just watering at the top, water finds its way through the system right down the bottom.

This system is becoming so prevalent that it is being incorporated into whole apartment blocks, internal and external walls of hotels and offices and home developments.

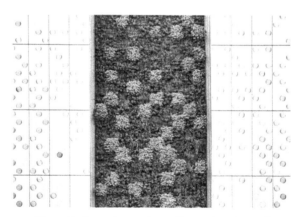

Figure 19. A very interesting wall on a shopping mall in Wroclaw.

As an unexpected side benefit, it has now been discovered that having a wall of green material provides a building with excellent insulation against both heat and sound. Another surprise benefit is that it dramatically cuts down graffiti because the graffiti 'artists' are no longer tempted by the blank canvas a bare wall offered.

4

A LOOK AT SOME ADVANCED CROPS FOR RAISED BEDS

In the first book of this series, we looked at growing some of the plants that are most commonly consumed by the home gardener. In this chapter, we are going to kick this up a notch and instead focus on some of the plants you may not typically have considered or had thought might be too difficult.

These plants may not be something you would ordinarily consume on a daily basis but would perhaps have purchased from time to time, either when the price was right or to add some variety to your diet. With your growing medium so easy to control, I am hoping that plants that were once thought of as something to eat every now and then, might now be grown more widely.

Figure 20. Freshly picked sunkissed vegetables.

CELERY:

Let's face facts; celery can be a temperamental plant even in the best of scenarios. As you will see, the raised bed option will help overcome many common problems when growing this plant, but you need to balance that out against the fact that global warming is making things harder. Big commercial growers tend to produce this crop in tunnels that often incorporate air temperature control. Although that means they can control the climate, they are not able to produce plants that are as tasty as real homegrown celery.

Figure 21. Homegrown celery plant.

The list of problems that celery poses to the home grower can seem somewhat overwhelming. They include bolting (at the drop of a hat), black heart, brittle or bitter leaves, too many leaves or they can just be too tough. With a pedigree like that, one solution is to say "Fine, I'll just buy a bunch next time I'm down the supermarket".

I want to urge you to be a little more adventurous here. Firstly, you will grow as a gardener even if you fail; secondly, you will eventually overcome the most common problems. Finally, and this is most important, once you master this plant, you will be able to casually give some to other gardeners who will probably have gone down this path and given up. I'm not suggesting that you boast here, but you should know that opportunity exists.

Celery is fussy about temperature and even when you have perfect raised beds, this is one little fly that nature is still able to drop into your ointment. If temperatures bounce up and down too much, celery panics and bolts. Bolting occurs when a plant says to itself "I'm going to die. I must produce offspring quickly." It then produces flowers and focuses all its attention on setting seed rather than on producing luscious green leaves.

If there is a risk of night temperatures dropping below 4.5° Celsius (40°F) then celery will be tempted to bolt. If you have grown your plants from seed indoors, or bought in seedlings, hold them back until you are sure that the night time temperature will not fall below this. Because you are using a raised bed, it should be easy enough to put in a tunnel over part of the bed using hoops, and it will be simpler to keep temperatures more stable. This will also mean that there is some shade during the hottest time of the day and you, therefore, reduce that effect where temperatures bounce up and down which celery hates.

If your plant does show signs of bolting, then cut off the early flowers and this may encourage it to focus more energy on the leaves. Also, harvest some leaves from the plant which should then encourage it to produce more foliage. Even if your plant does bolt and gets away from you, all is not lost. The leaves can still be used in soups, or the plants can be left to do their own thing. They will get tall and covered in flowers which will be a boon for the local bees and butterflies. When fellow gardeners visit, you can tell them you have grown these plants to help the environment.

Another dreaded problem that makes many gardeners shudder is called black heart. The inner leaves die, and those that remain are tough. This is usually an indication of a lack of calcium in the soil and is one problem that carefully managed raised beds shouldn't present. Because the raised bed gardener is so diligent about adding well-rotted compost his soil is generally not prone to this problem. Topdressing with more compost helps ensure this never becomes an issue and regulates soil temperature. Some varieties have been bred to resist this problem. You might try 'Verde Pascal' or 'Conquistador'. If the leaves are cracked, brittle, or are simply too tough, there are two probable reasons. There is a Boron deficiency, or the soil is getting too hot. Boron deficiency is unlikely as you have managed the soil so thoroughly, but just in case, add plenty of fertilizer tea. A more likely culprit is that the soil is becoming too hot. Ideally, you want to time your planting so that you can harvest in the autumn and avoid the hottest of the summer. Also, six hours of sun is enough for this plant so place them where they will get some shade from taller plants such as tomatoes or use that tunnel covered in shade cloth.

If you are growing your plants from seed, you will need to start them indoors or in the greenhouse ten weeks before you intend to plant them out. That is a long time to be nurturing seedlings, so time this so that they go out as the hottest months draw to a close. If it is too hot, hold them back until conditions are not so harsh. You will be best placed to be able to assess local conditions, but as all gardeners are learning, those predictions are becoming harder to make. This is a plant where the choice of variety can be really crucial. Speak to your local nurseryman or members of your garden club to see what varieties have worked well in the past.

EGGPLANT:

This is a great plant to grow, especially if you are a cook. An adventurous chef can do wonders with this plant, and they are often quite expensive at local supermarkets or greengrocers so it is definitely one to try. If you have become addicted to growing heirloom seeds, there are numerous varieties of both shape and colour that you simply won't see in most commercial outlets.

Figure 22. Eggplant or aubergine makes for delicious vegetarian recipes.

All eggplants make handsome additions to the garden as well as providing a delicious crop. They are cousins of the tomato, the pepper and the potato (as well as deadly nightshade but let's not go there).

Start seeds indoors and plant out as seedlings only once you are sure that the last of the frosts have passed. As with most seedlings, they should be hardened off gradually before being planted into their final position. They need full sun and will take sixty to ninety days to reach harvest stage depending on local conditions. Ideally, they need a day time temperature of 26° Celsius (80°F), but night-time temperatures shouldn't go too much below 18°c (65°F).

Stake them when you plant them and feed them every two weeks with an organic liquid feed. If you want enormous fruits, then leave only two or three per plant. If you are happy with slightly smaller fruit, then you will get more per plant if you let them all grow. Pick them when they are ready to eat.

Figure 23. Graffiti eggplant, also called "Sicilian eggplant", gets its name from its purple and white stripes.

They don't store well but you get a little extra shelf life if you clip them off with an inch or so of stem still attached.

If you are planning on saving the seed, then you will need to keep one of the fruits until it has gone past the edible stage and has started to dry out. Grate the base of the fruit over a bowl of water using a vegetable grater. The seed will sink and can then be dried for use the following season.

The reason this fruit can be difficult to grow is that they are susceptible to pests who love them as much as gardeners do. As we are organic gardeners, we are not able to defend ourselves as easily as those who are happy to just blast pests with toxic chemicals. That does not mean, however, that we are defenceless.

The most prevalent pest on these plants is the Colorado beetle.He is an easy to identify little critter with a golden shell and ten pronounced black stripes.

Figure 24. The colorado Beetle.

If you are observing your plants closely regularly, then you will see him before he can become established. They can be picked off by hand and destroyed and the plant sprayed with vegetable soap or neem for good measure. Another common pest that is more difficult to spot is the spider mite. These creatures are almost microscopic but their presence will be given away by white spots on the leaves and fine silky webbing on the undersides.

Early infestations can be resolved simply by spraying the underside of the leaves with a harsh jet of water. If they persist then use a garlic spray or some neem oil.

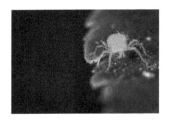

Figure 25. The Spider mite.

The other pest that blights this plant is the flea beetle. These tiny jumping beetles have a similar appearance to fleas and chew holes in the leaves which leave the plant looking like someone had a go at it with a shotgun.

Figure 26. The Flea beetle.

seventy percent neem oil spray will typically deal with infestations if they are caught early. Further into this book series, we will take a more in-depth look at some of the organic methods for dealing with common garden pests.

CAULIFLOWER:

Cauliflowers are loaded with anti-oxidants and teeming with vitamin C. Despite these health benefits, they languished for many years in the background along with those vegetables that were only eaten occasionally and sometimes even reluctantly. And then came the arrival of the popular low carb diet and suddenly demand for this vegetable went through the roof.

Figure 27. The cauliflower white compact head is also known as "curd".

Where once the cauliflower had been seen as lacking taste and only edible if smothered in a creamy white sauce, top chefs were now promoting it and offering a wide range of previously unconsidered cooking possibilities. Today this humble vegetable is frequently used as a replacement for the higher calorie potato and is now being served mashed, roasted in a marinade and even barbecued. The ketogenic diet might have knocked the calorie out of fashion, but it has certainly placed the cauliflower in vogue.

A member of the brassica family, cauliflowers like a well-fed soil and so will thrive in your raised beds. To ensure a reliable succession, sow seed in March, early May and again in early June. You have the option of sowing directly into the ground or into modules. I would suggest sowing the first two crops in modules and the last directly into the ground when the weather is a bit more reliable. When using modules, sow the seed an inch deep and two to a module. They grow quickly and will be ready to plant out in around four weeks. Where two seedlings appear in a module, select the stronger of the pair and pinch out the other. Don't attempt to pull out the one that doesn't make the cut as you will damage the roots of the plant you want to keep. Plants grown in modules will get leggy if they have too much heat or too much light so grow them on a moderately warm windowsill and keep them damp but not wet.

Like most seedlings started indoors, they will need to be hardened off before planting out. To get really big heads, space your seedlings two feet apart. In the more confined space of a raised bed, you can keep them closer together, but the heads will be smaller. It becomes a matter of personal preference whether you want giant plants or not. Because they are a little sensitive to drying out, it is important to either plant them in the evening or water in straight after planting.

Several pests are attracted to cauliflower and have been since way before the low carb diet came into fashion. Perhaps the fact that you seldom see an obese cabbage root fly is testimony to just how effective this trendy diet can be. These pesky little creatures look a bit like a house fly but are more of a grey colour. They like to lay their eggs at the base of your plants and when the eggs hatch the maggots crawl down and feast on the roots. The first thing the gardener knows about this is when his plant starts to wilt, and the leaves turn a bluish-grey colour. By then it is usually too late and the plant quickly succumbs.

There are a couple of ways to deal with this that conform to organic principals. The most effective is to cover the plants with fine mesh, sometimes called bio mesh, which denies access to the fly. It is not a very pretty sight, but as long as the mesh is in place your plants are safe.

Figure 28. Garden mesh is the best protection against pests without using pesticides.

The second method is to make plant collars. These are simple collars, cut from roofing felt or carpet underlay that fit around the stem of the plant and prevent the maggots from getting to the roots. It is not quite as effective as the mesh method but is far less obtrusive visually. I would suggest that you experiment with both and see what system work best for you.

Another cauliflower connoisseur is the cabbage white caterpillar. These are the progeny of the rather attractive cabbage white butterfly. The caterpillars are green, and there is no such thing as one cabbage white caterpillar. They tend to emerge in thuggish gangs that can decimate the leaves of an entire plant overnight. Close observation is your optimum weapon here. The butterfly lays her yellow eggs in batches on the underside of the leaves and, provided you are looking for them, they are relatively easy to spot.

You can then simply rub them between thumb and forefinger, and the whole problem is avoided. This is another one of those instances where raised beds can really make your life that little bit easier.

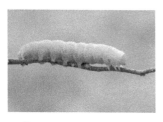

Figure 29. The Cabbage white caterpillar.

Not having to bend as much makes the egg hunt far less like a Pilates stretch class. If you are using bio netting against the cabbage fly, you will, of course, eliminate this pest at the same time.

The cabbage whitefly is a type of aphid who also does his best to make your gardening life that little bit more of a challenge. Like all aphids, these are sap-sucking insects that inject their tiny proboscises into the leaf and feed on the sap. They secrete a sticky substance politely referred to as honeydew, and this can easily contribute to fungal diseases. Ants love honeydew and will actually farm the aphid by carrying them to different parts of the plant. Often it is the ant that first alerts the gardener to the aphid's presence. Compared to other pests, these guys are wimps and can easily be blasted out of existence with a hose or squirt of vegetable soap. Once you have learned to spot them, you will be able to pick them off before they can become established mercilessly.

Clubroot is a disease that commonly affects cauliflower but is much more of a problem when plants are grown in the open ground than in raised beds. It thrives in infected soil, and as the raised bed soil is normally of such high quality, incidents of it in these environments are far less common. It manifests itself through reddish-purple leaves and weak growth. When the plant is pulled up, there are knobbly lumps on the roots that are a sure indicator as to the causes of this problem. It can be avoided by choosing resistant varieties. If you do have infected plants, they should not be added to the compost, and the top layer of the soil should be replaced.

GLOBE ARTICHOKE:

These are plants that are both delicious to eat and easy to grow. Also, they provide a wonderful architectural element to the garden because of their impressive form. They are perennial, so they don't need to be replaced every year. With all of these attributes going for them, you would think that this was one plant that would be far more widely grown by the home gardener. The reason for the lack of take up is that many people simply aren't sure what to do with them from a culinary point of view, and so they are simply overlooked.

Start seeds off in trays in late March to early April and plant them half an inch deep. As soon as they are large enough to handle, they can be hardened off and moved to their new permanent home. Normally they will have about five or six leaves by then. Bear in mind they are both tall and will be around for some years, so put some

Figure 30. Artichokes are the flower buds of the plant which are edible before the flowers come into bloom.

thought into where you plant them. If you are lucky, you should get a few flowers at the end of the first year. Don't worry if there are not many, they will go on producing the following year, and flowering will be far more prolific. In autumn, mulch their bases with compost or straw.

These plants are not very prone to pests but keep an eye out for the odd mob of marauding aphids. Blast them off with water or vegetable soap depending on your weapon of choice. When young they are favoured by snails and slugs, but hopefully, the raised bed helps keep these guys in check. Flowers can be simply snipped off in July or August when they are the size of a golf ball. This will give you the first crop and encourage the plant to produce a second. Boil the flower until it is soft enough to easily remove the scale-like leaves and then fry the hearts in butter. It really is that simple and they are delicious.

As they get older, plants become woody and start to produce fewer flowers. Lift them with a garden fork and divide them to encourage new fresh growth. Good varieties include 'Purple Sicilian' and 'Green Globe'.

PARSNIPS:

Parsnips are a popular root crop, but they can be a little tricky. This stems from the fact that, unlike carrots which may look somewhat similar, parsnips must be grown using fresh seed.

Purchase seed each season and check the date on the packet to ensure that what you are buying is in date. Generally, you will end up with more seed than you can use and it is very tempting to keep this and hope that you can get a second sowing the following year. The success rate will be so low that you are far better off just giving the seed away to another gardener while it is still viable. One of the main reasons that people believe this to be a problematic crop is that they attempt to use old seed.

Plant seeds about three inches apart in drills that are one inch deep. The seeds are incredibly light, so it is probably best not to try this on a windy day. Cover the seeds and water in lightly. This should be done in early May. One month later when the plants are starting to germinate, thin out every second plant. This ensures that they have plenty of space to grow without competing with one another. If you leave this part of the operation too late, you risk damaging the roots of those plants that you want to keep.

Figure 31. Raw parsnips.

Don't feed them during as this will lead to leaf growth at the expense of the root. The best time to harvest is just after the first frosts of the season. They should lift easily and should be large and healthy.

People planting directly into the ground often plant their parsnips in toilet rolls. This ensures that the gardener gets strong straight growth and the roots aren't diverted when they hit stones or other underground obstacles. By the time the toilet roll disintegrates, the roots are strong enough to push their way past anything that might get in their way. In the raised bed environment, the soil is normally so conditioned that it is not really necessary but feel free to use this technique if you feel your growing medium is too stony.

SWEET POTATOES:

Another delicious garden plant that is only really being discovered by home gardeners. The sweet potato is grown from slips which you can purchase but tend to be expensive when you can find them. They are so easy to produce yourself that once you have done this, you will wonder why anyone ever buys them.

Figure 32. Fifthy shades of sweet.

Mound some of your planting mix to a height of eight inches high and twelve inches wide. Leave three feet between the rows. This means that you can comfortably get two rows in a four-foot-wide raised bed. You can now plant your rooted slips every twelve inches along each of the mounds.

Unlike ordinary potatoes, they don't grow as bushes but as sprawling vines. Though they can take up a lot of space and would probably account for a whole bed, they are attractive, especially if left hanging from a vertical planter.

Figure 33. Sweet potato harvest.

They should be planted out in spring and will be ready to harvest by late summer. The vines will dry out when the potatoes are ready, and you should stop watering at that stage. Leave them dry for the last three weeks before digging them up. They can easily be lifted with a fork but avoid digging too close to the plants so you don't stab the roots. Throughout the growing season, they need to be kept evenly moist. This is best done by letting the top two inches of the soil go dry. Test regularly to ensure that the soil surface is dry but that the subsoil is still moist. You can do this by merely poking your finger two inches into the soil and feeling for dampness.

To produce your own slips, cut one of your potatoes in half and stand it in an old ice cream container with an inch of water in the bottom. Top up the water from time to time so that the base of the potato does not become dry. Stand the container on a windowsill, and after a month you will start to see shoots growing from the sides of your parent potatoes.

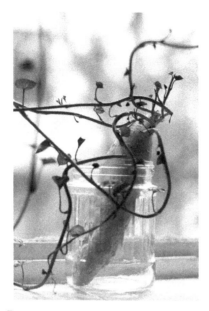

Figure 34. Starting a young sweet potato slip.

Once these are around twelve inches high, then simply snap them off the edge of the potatoes and stand each one in a jar of water. All the base of the stem that is submerged will start to produce roots. When the roots are established, then you can pot up your new plant into a pot filled with potting soil. Continue to grow them indoors for another month and then plant them out in May. They will need to be kept under a fleece for the first week or two to harden off safely. You should be able to harvest in November. Expect to get roughly four to six slips per half parent potato.

SWEET CORN:

The next slightly unusual crop we're going to look at is sweet corn. Scientists believe that human beings have been growing corn for the last 10,000 years. It was developed from the grass 'teosinte' in Mexico, although what we eat today is very different from the corn of that era. You will need to make sure when you buy your seed, that you purchase a variety that has been designated as sweet corn. There is corn designed for popcorn, flour and animal feed, and none of these will prove delicious when served on the dining table.

Corn makes up a large part of the staple diet in many parts of the world. Corn, or maize as it is sometimes called, is grown far more widely than either wheat or rice. Although it makes up the staple diet in many places, most production is intended for animal feed and increasingly for ethanol as a fuel additive. In fact, in some parts of Europe, many people are still suspicious of eating corn as a vegetable as they are far more familiar using at it as duck or cattle fodder. This is mainly because they have not encountered the sweeter cultivars of this particular crop. What they have been growing and feeding their livestock for decades, is a tough and unsavoury variety of maize.

Figure 35. Kid's favourite.

Corn is a warm-weather crop. Ideally, it prefers temperatures of between 20 and 30° C. It does not like to drop below 10° C at any time. It is an ideal crop to plant into beds after lettuce or some of your early leafy vegetables. Before planting, lightly dig over the bed with a fork while at the same time digging in some manure or rich compost. Traditionally in parts of the world where corn was widely consumed, it was grown on top of fish carcasses which would have provided plenty of nutrients. The stalks were used as a climbing support for beans and the shade that the plants provided created a cool growing environment for pumpkins. This multi-cropping method is still very much a part of the permaculture movement. Whilst this is still a viable option, I would recommend that you grow your sweet corn in a bed dedicated solely to this crop, at least until you are familiar with it.

When growing corn, it is a good idea to start some off in containers in the house four weeks before they are due to be planted out in early May. Come May, providing that the weather is warm enough, plant out your seedlings, but at the same time plant some seeds directly into the bed to provide a succession crop once you have reaped the first one. Three weeks after you have planted the seeds and the seedlings, you can sow a second crop of seeds. This should provide you with a steady succession of sweet corn throughout the summer season. You need to plant your plants about 12 inches apart. Any closer together than that and the plants will be shading one another and rubbing together, and they will not perform well. Seeds should be planted in rows at a depth of one and a half inches. Sow two or three seeds per hole and then snip off weaker plants once they come through. There's an argument as to whether to grow in blocks or rows. This is because, unlike most crops which are pollinated by insects, corn is wind-pollinated. The pollen is carried on the flowering heads of the male plants. The silky tassel on the cob is the female plant that will need to come into contact with the wind-born pollen to provide fruit on the cob. By keeping your crop in blocks, the argument goes, you increase the chances of the pollen reaching the female plant. I have not found any particular difference in yield, whether in rows or blocks.

Bear in mind that corn cannot withstand cold of any kind and is very thirsty. You will need to water regularly. It does not need to be fed during the growing season but should be planted into any already rich bed. Remember that corn is a grass and the last thing you want is for it to grow tall and leggy which it will do if you give it too much fertilizer. Each succession that you plant should take about 10 to 12 weeks to ripen. Ensure that your last succession isn't still trying to mature when the weather becomes cold.

You can tell when the cobs are ripe because the ends become more rounded and the silk becomes brown. As you reap the last of the ripened cobs from each successive planting, you can remove the stems and leaves and add them to your compost heap. This will allow both space and light for the crops that are following. You do not need to reap all of the cobs as soon as they become ripe. You can leave them on the plant for several days but do not leave them for too long, or they will become floury and eventually dry out.

Figure 36. Green corn plant standing tall.

Whilst corn is a wonderful crop both to eat and to grow, you need to bear in mind that it takes up a lot of space and is very thirsty. It would help if you also considered that because of its height (plants can reach 1.8 meters tall), it will cast plenty of shade which may affect other crops that you wish to grow. Another thing to consider is that corn is a shallow-rooted plant. This means that you need to consider the wind in your area.

If you live in a wind-blown place, you will need to plant your crop in a sheltered position. If you don't, the wind might knock your plants down. If you have raised beds that are high, the full-grown plants will be at quite a height. One way to reduce this wind vulnerability will be to use smaller cultivars that remain relatively small though this will result in a smaller yield of cobs.

BROCCOLI:

Over recent years broccoli has gone through something of a renaissance primarily due to its reputation as being a superfood. This is because of its high vitamin carrying capacity and a high content of anti-cancer properties. Although I cannot vouch for its efficacy is a superfood, I do know that broccoli is one of these crops where the homegrown variety is simply far more delicious than anything you will find in the supermarket. What is more, is that supermarket broccoli has become quite expensive and this is an added incentive to produce your own. There are many different varieties of broccoli, and you're going to need to experiment to find out which ones best suits your requirements and growing conditions. Whichever variety you opt for, I recommend that you cultivate and grow them in containers for eight weeks before planting them out. The tender seedlings are just too tempting for slugs and snails to risk sowing directly into your bed.

Sow two seeds per cell and then thin to one once you can see which of the pair is going to be weaker. Keep your seedlings on a windowsill or in a greenhouse until they're about 5 inches high. Once a week you can feed them with a liquid feed so that they are in prime condition when you plant them.

They will need to be planted in a bed that receives full sun or a little bit of shade. You should plant each seedling 1 foot apart in rows 18 inches apart. As soon as they go into the ground, you should cover your seedlings with netting. Being members of the brassica family, these plants are a delicacy to pests such as cabbage butterfly and cabbage fly. You will need to keep them netted in taller plants or until they are well enough established and their leaves are tough enough to resist the threats.

Broccoli produces a healthy head which I'm sure you are familiar with after having seen them in your local supermarket. As soon as the head is large enough cut it off with a knife and it is ready to prepare. If you leave it on the plant for too long, it will turn yellow as each of little buds that make up the head is a flower bud and you need to harvest before the flowers open. Leave the remainder of the plant in the ground, and it will continue to produce smaller sprouts that you can cut off and eat.

Figure 37. Lieutenant Broccoli grown in a raised garden bed.

The softer leaves that surround the head are perfectly edible and can be treated and cooked in the same way that Kale can. Another trick to make your harvest go further and avoid waste is to peel the hard stem that the head is carried on and cook that in the same way as you would regular broccoli.

One of the common problems that beginners have when growing this vegetable is that they have lovely healthy-looking plants that simply fail to produce a head of any kind. This is most commonly due to the fact that they have not given the plant sufficient water. Broccoli is another of those crops that require a great deal of water to produce well. Bolting can also be an issue, but if you see the head starting to turn yellow, then cut it off immediately. You should be able to collect some edible material from the head but, more importantly, the plant will now start to produce more sprouts, and your efforts won't have been wasted.

Figure 38. Romanesco Broccoli variety.

Figure 39. Purple broccoli flower.

Some people sow seed directly into the beds after April. The reason that I don't do this is that the seedlings are so vulnerable to attack by pests. If that is not an issue in your garden, then you might prefer this method than going to all the effort of growing indoors in modules. I would still recommend the use of netting. Finally, there are many different varieties of broccoli. These include differences in shape, size and colour, but more importantly, differences in timing. You will need to experiment with early and late varieties and see which provide you with the best results. They grow well with Kale which is yet another superfood.

MELONS:

There is something about growing your own melons that just says that you have arrived as a gardener. They are not all that difficult to produce but people always think that they are and is it really your job to correct that misconception? Not only will they give you instant kudos in the word of gardeners, but their fruit also provides one of the most delicious of summer rewards and costs a small fortune when purchased at the local greengrocer.

Figure 40. Homegrown watermelons are one of the real sweet treat pleasures of summer.

If you are going to grow melons in a raised bed, then you will want to climb them up a trellis. Something like watermelon can spread 15 feet in all directions and unless the gardener introduces some form of discipline, then a plant this vigorous can soon get out of control. With the ideal conditions that the raised bed provides, an uncontrolled melon will happily make your garden look like into a set from The Day of the Triffids. Also, it is not just what is above ground that is greedy for space. Below ground, the roots will be equally territorial. The trellis is the ideal answer to this problem but melons, and especially watermelons, can be really heavy so that trellis will need to be secure. It should also be high if the watermelon is your melon of choice. Seven feet will be just about high enough.

Melons need plenty of sun, and they have a long growing season. This means you will want to get them into the ground early but well after the last frosts. If you live in an area where the growing season is short and the soil is slow to warm up then cover the soil with black plastic to gain those crucial few degrees. You can also start your melons off in modules, but they are deep-rooted plants so this is not ideal.

The surest way to get a good result is to plant your seed directly into your bed. Unless your bed is enormous, then it is probably best to have one dedicated solely to melons because they like their space so much. That doesn't stop you growing an early crop before the melons go in and another autumn crop once they are harvested so that the bed remains highly productive overall.

Melons have a particularly long growing season as most of them originate in areas where long hot summers are the norm. As you are probably going to be cultivating in areas that are not quite ideal, you should choose your varieties with care. Traditional melons take 90 to 100 days to reach maturity. If you opt for a variety that is quicker growing, you can knock this down to 75 days. Not only will that make reaching maturity more likely, but it will also mean that you get your bed back earlier to sow another crop.

I have mentioned the importance of choosing your varieties with care several times in this chapter. It really can be a game-changer, especially in the raised bed arena where space is sometimes limited but the gardener still wants to maximize yields. Plant breeders have spent decades developing varieties with different traits such as dwarf varieties of maize, late or early broccoli or melons that fruit early. Learning which varieties that best suit your needs is essential because it really can make a difference to the yield that you can produce. That is one of the reasons that gardeners spend so long poring over seed catalogues. These can be invaluable when it comes to choosing what to plant. I tend to steer clear of seeds that have just come out and have yet to be proven in the field. Instead, I go for varieties that have been around for some time and have withstood the tests that the market imposes on them. With the advent of the internet, I am now able to research a particular variety and see what other gardeners have experienced. In this way, I am no longer reliant purely on the lyrical marketing descriptions provided by the seed merchant and can get a broader range of opinion.

Melons will need to be tied into the trellis as they grow. They do produce tendrils, but these plants are used to sprawling over the ground, and the tendrils won't hold to the trellis in the same way that peas or runner beans will.

A watermelon can grow as much as two feet per week so expect to be doing quite a lot of tying in. I generally let the main shoot keep growing upwards until it reaches the top of the trellis and I pinch out most of the side shoots to prevent things from becoming over-crowded.

Don't be in too much of a rush to cut back side shoots. You want to ensure that you have enough flowers to produce fruit so let the fruit start to develop before cutting out side shoots. This will cause more nutrients to go toward the fruit rather than side shoots. Ties will need to be soft because the plant's stems are quite fragile. Instead of using string as you would typically do for this job, consider strips of plastic or old nylon tights.

Figure 41. Cantaloupe grown on trellis.

It is not only the vines that will have to be tied into the trellis. When the plant starts to produce fruit, these too will need to be supported. Every gardener seems to have his favourite system for holding up melons. Common choices include netting, old T-shirts, nylon stockings and voluptuous bras. Quite which method you opt for is down to you, as long as whatever is supporting the melon is tied securely to the trellis. You will need to recognize that your melon is going to gain in both weight and size and the tension that this applies must be suspended by the trellis rather than the vine, which could well break.

Initially, the vine will produce many fruits and it might be tempting to keep them all in the hopes of securing a bumper crop. Unfortunately, life is not so kind. Some of the fruit will wither naturally and some you will need to clip off. Wait a while to see which ones show the most potential and then decide if you want quantity or size. Don't go for more than four fruit per plant as they will not mature well. If you want a giant fruit, then snip off all but one but expect to have to support a very heavy watermelon.

Finally, knowing when to harvest your melons can be a bit of a trick because they all have their distinctive signs to show that they are ripe. Watermelons have a tendril growing on the stem immediately behind the melon itself. Don't break this off because this is the perfect tell-tale as to the fruit's ripeness. When that little tendril curls up and goes brown, you can harvest in safety.

The cantaloupe, on the other hand, will change from green to tan in colour, and this tells you that it is nearing perfection. If you gently tug the fruit and it comes away from the stem, then you are fine. If it doesn't let go without a fight, then leave it on the vine for another day or two.

The honeydew rind will turn from green to white or yellow. Unlike the cantaloupe, it will not come away from the vine easily and will need to be snipped off. It will then continue to ripen in a cool room for the next few days.

Figure 42. Despite their name, honeydew are not loaded with sugar.

KALE:

Kale is one of those vegetables that are not only nutritious but also brings with it an attractive stately appearance. We have been eating Kale from more than 2000 years, and it is another one of those so-called superfoods. Unlike most vegetables, it will tolerate as little as 4 hours of sun per day. It can also be sown directly into your beds 4 to 6 weeks before the last frosts. This plant takes eight or nine weeks to reach maturity. If you want to eat it raw in salads, then you can snap off a few of the younger leaves earlier than that.

Figure 43. Kale is one of the healthiest superfoods.

Seeds should be planted half an inch deep and 12 inches apart. Once they have germinated then mulch the ground with compost and feed the plants once per month with compost tea. They need to be well watered once per week in dry conditions.

This plant is from the same family as broccoli, and many gardeners choose to grow these plants together. Part of the reason for this is that both plants are susceptible to the same pests, these being cabbage caterpillars and cabbage fly. As the two plants go well together and as they are both attacked by the same pests, it makes sense to grow them in the same bed because then you can net both plants at the same time. They also share the same growing requirements. If you do decide to grow these two plants together, make sure that you opt for varieties that will reach a similar height. If you don't do this, the taller plant will dominate and steal from the smaller one.

Kale leaves can be very tough, and although the younger leaves can be eaten raw, mature leaves will need to be cooked. There are a variety of ways of doing this including frying them as chips as a replacement for the potato chip or adding them to stir-fries, soups and stews. The centre stems will need to be removed because they tend to be extremely tough and are almost inedible. Kale can be stored in a plastic bag in the refrigerator with most of the air squeezed out of the bag. If the leaves start to turn yellow, then it is probably time you added it to the compost heap.

ARUGULA:

This is a wonderful cool weather plant that you may be more familiar with under its common name of rocket. Some gardening books refer to it as roquette but in my opinion, this is just downright pretentious (unless you happen to be reading in French).

This crop will produce profuse amounts of leaves if it is happy, and this, in turn, makes me happy because its sharp spicy leaves really add something to salads. Because it prefers cool conditions, it is best cultivated in early spring or early autumn. It can be sown directly into the ground or started off in containers.

To grow it in the ground, make shallow drills with the edge of a trowel and then sprinkle the fine seed directly from the packet to create an almost continuous row of seed. Rows should be spaced about four inches apart. Cover the seed lightly with soil and then water in gently. Don't bother to thin the seedlings once they appear as this plant can tolerate a bit of crowding and you will probably consume it fairly quickly.

Figure 44. Commonly known as Rocket, Arugula is native to the Mediterranean region.

You can also sow seeds in modules and start them off on a sunny windowsill. They will germinate in four to five days. Plant them out when the first roots start to appear through the bottom of the module.

Once established, the plants will need to be kept moist and not allowed to dry out or they will bolt. As with many cool-weather plants, bolting is something you will need to keep an eye out for. If they do show signs of trying to set seed, then harvest them immediately and you should be able to salvage some edible material.

They only need four to five hours of sun per day, so if you have a bed that gets a little shade, this will be the place to plant them. They are prone to attack from flea beetles which will pepper the leaves with tiny holes. These are still edible but it weakens the plant. To overcome this issue, the easiest and most organically effective way is to cover the plants with netting and only open it up when you are harvesting.

BRUSSELS SPROUTS:

There can be few vegetables that generate more of a like them or hate them attitude than the good old brussels sprout. I won't enter into that debate here other than to say they are a great crop to plant in raised beds but that they can provide challenges for the gardener. They need a long growing season, and they tend to be top-heavy so you will need to provide them with stakes.

To further complicate matters, they like to be kept moist, and they don't like the weather to be too warm. If you are not a true fan of this vegetable, I suspect that you are already seeing this plant as having enough get-out clauses for you to ignore them altogether.

Challenging though they may be, they are still worth the effort. They are high in vitamins for starters. A small handful of them contains more vitamin C than four oranges, and they store well. Because of their long growing season, you will almost definitely need to start them off indoors or undercover somewhere. Once your seedlings are established, they can be planted out, but they will need to be kept about eighteen inches apart. Get your stakes in early, so you don't risk damaging the root system at a later stage.

Figure 45. Love them or hate them ?

Most gardeners plant seed in mid-March indoors and then get them into the ground by early May. This allows them to get established before the hotter weather really sets in. As members of the brassica family, they are prone to attack from the usual suspects; the cabbage white butterfly and the cabbage fly. Net them as soon as they go into the ground as they are at their most vulnerable. Another thing to remember about all members of the brassica family is that they like plenty of nitrogen. If you have been managing your beds well, this shouldn't be an issue but try not to plant them in beds that have just produced a brassica crop.

They can be grown with cabbage as the two plants have similar growing requirements and the difference in heights make them ideal growing partners. As they become taller some of the lower leaves can be removed. This encourages the plant to direct more nutrients towards the sprouts and also facilitates air and light getting to them. One tip is to cut the lower leaves before they get too tough and then they can be cooked and eaten like cabbage.

Continue removing the lower leaves with either secateurs or a knife as the plant grows. It really only needs a clump of leaves at the top to be able to photosynthesize effectively. As they are heavy feeders, give them a watering with nettle tea or liquid fish food every three weeks and keep them well mulched with compost. They require 110 to 120 days to get to a stage where they are ready for harvest and often this will take place only after the first frosts have struck. It is widely believed that this early frost exposure improves the taste of the sprouts.

The lower sprouts will reach a harvestable size earlier than those higher up the plant, but they can be harvested gradually so those higher ones will have time to reach a better size. Some plants may produce relatively small sprouts. If you snap off the top two inches of the plant, the sprouts should grow larger. That top piece that you snap off can be cooked and is one of the most delicious parts of the whole plant.

Figure 46. Brussels sprouts harvesting.

If you are living in a warm climate, then the best time to plant them out is in early autumn. Look for a winter growing variety as these will be hardier. This will generate a late winter harvest. They can withstand frost, so they make a good winter crop. Just before the first frosts, pinch out the top inch or two of the growing stems. Again, this will encourage the plant to focus its growth lower down and will result in larger sprouts. A good harvest would see you getting approximately fifty sprouts per plant.

With a winter crop, you will be able to remove the netting as soon as the weather cools and the pests go into retreat.

KALETTES:

In the world of superfoods, kalettes are the new kid on the block. There are now so many of these so-called superfoods that if you are growing them all you might want to think about wearing a cape. Kalettes are a cross between brussels sprouts and Kale.

Instead of the sprouts springing out up the stem of the plant, you will find small florets which look like miniature kale plants. They are grown in very much the same way as brussels sprouts with all of the same growing requirements though they require less space. Like brussels sprouts, they come in different varieties, and you will need to choose one that corresponds with your growing temperatures and the time of year that you wish to plant.

Once the small florets of leaves are harvested, they can be cooked and treated as winter greens. Those that are not brussels sprouts fans will be pleased to know that the taste is more like Kale than it is like sprouts.

Figure 47. Kalettes have a sweet, nutty flavour.

With both brussels sprouts and kalettes, once you have harvested, cut off the plant at the base of the stem and allow what is still below ground to decay back into the soil where it will simply add to the richness of the soil.

OTHER FRUIT:

During the course of this book and its predecessor, much of the focus of raised bed gardening has been toward the production of vegetables. This system indeed lends itself to growing vegetables, but I like to think of the raised bed garden as being a more holistic production zone. Many gardeners today, are trying to reach a point where they are as self-sufficient as possible. In order to do this, we need to think about fruits as well as vegetables. Whilst melons may be something of a luxury; there are plenty of other fruits that can be produced by the home gardener that will increase his productivity and self-sufficiency. Although much of this fruit is not really dependent on their raised bed system, planting fruit trees and bushes may still be something you want to consider when you design your garden.

Later in this series, we will be looking at fruit in greater depth, but at the moment, I simply want you to understand that there is room in the raised bed garden system to incorporate fruit. Cane fruits such as blueberries, thornless blackberries, raspberries and red currants all thrive in raised beds, but you can go further than that. The worry most beginner gardeners have is that tree fruits such as apples, pears and quince will get too big for the space allotted to them and cast shade over the raised beds.

It is entirely possible to purchase and plant dwarf varieties of fruit or to train your fruit trees to grow along wires in a system that is known as espalier cultivation. Using this system, the branches of the chosen tree would be tied onto support wires that run along a fence, for example. The fruit tree is then rigidly disciplined to grow and produce fruit parallel to the fence and does not need to impinge on the space allotted to the raised bed section of the garden. Done correctly, this can also become a beautiful frame for any garden. As an alternative to the regular espalier system, both pears and apples can be trained as stepovers providing the correct varieties are chosen. A stepover fruit tree is one that is trained to grow along a low wire and produce fruit at the height of little more than one foot.

All of these options that we will look at in more depth later in the series. I mention it at this stage merely to encourage you to think or your raised bed garden as being more than just for the production of vegetables.

5

EXTENDING THE GROWING SEASON

I n both this book and its predecessor, An Introduction to Raised Bed Gardening, I have touched on the subject of self-sufficiency. I have been careful to point out that these methods might lead you toward self-sufficiency. Going fully self-sufficient is a far more complicated matter. Growing all of your own fruit and vegetables is demanding work and a more realistic aspiration would be to produce the majority of the fruit and vegetables that you and your family consume. There is a reason for this, and it affects even the most dedicated gardeners.

The lean season or the hungry gap, are terms used to refer to that period between late winter and early summer. It is that punitive time where you have consumed all of the produce you stored, canned and froze the previous year but before you are able to harvest anything from the current season. It is not a new phenomenon and it has blighted gardeners and farmers since we first started to sow the seed to soil.

Producing crops twelve months of the year is difficult and becomes something of a juggling act that can really test a gardener's skills. It is, however, gratifying pulling something edible from the ground at a time when the earth appears barren and devoid of nourishment. In this chapter, we will be looking at some of the tricks to prolong the growing season. I am still not promising that you will never need to venture into the greengrocer's again, but you will be in a position to maximise the productivity of those raised beds that you worked so hard to install. I always think it is a shame when I see beds lying fallow that could, with a little effort and ingenuity, be producing something useful for the kitchen. Lean season beds may not be the lush eye-catching affairs that they are in the gentler months, but they can still deliver healthy produce.

To maximise your yield, you are going to need to get the hang of the different varieties of vegetables available. Many of them will have attributes that can dramatically extend the growing season. Seed merchants and nurserymen will often offer varieties that are early producers, late producers or are hardier than the more familiar seeds and vegetables that we commonly use. This can open the door to producing crops outside of what we consider the normal seasonal range. Many gardeners ignore these seeds because they have their traditional favourites or because they have become used to growing certain plants at a specific time of year. A gardener only has to pay attention to what is printed on the seed packet or in the catalogue to discover a whole new world of seeds that can vastly increase annual yields. To add to this, we are now blessed with access to a vast treasure trove of information via the internet, and it is worth starting to become familiar with tapping into this resource.

For the gardener wanting to maximise his harvest, planning becomes essential. You will need to know in advance what crops are going to go into the ground when, and at what time they are going to be harvested. Once these plans are fully developed, the gardener will be able to harvest and then plant successively so that the beds are never being left in an unproductive state. Obviously, there might be slight hiccups in these plans due to weather and environmental factors, but by and large, the gardener will have a good idea of what will be happening and when. Raised beds greatly facilitate these opportunities because the gardener is so easily able to ensure that the soil is always in tip-top condition.

A well-developed garden plan will include what seeds or plants are going into the ground and when and what varieties they are going to be. It will also incorporate what seedlings are growing in the house or greenhouse. There was a time when creating garden plans of this depth and detail would take a gardener days or even weeks of in-depth research and study. Today there are easy to use apps that take much of the hard work out of this vital job. Despite this, however, the gardener is still going to have to build up their own knowledge because no app or planning book is going offer the kind of information that actual hands-on gardening provides.

Figure 48. Cozy greenhouse.

At the end of the planning process, you should come away with a month by month garden plan, which you would be well advised to print out. That way you can not only refer to it regularly but also make notes so that the following season you will have a road map of where you are going and what did and didn't work the previous season. Over time, you will build up a wealth of knowledge which will prove invaluable to you as a gardener. No book or app will ever be able to provide the kind of in-depth information specific to your garden that this experience will. The only other way to short cut this system is to beg, steal or borrow information from more experienced gardeners in your local area. Many new gardeners can be a little shy about doing this, but I can't reiterate enough how much I was helped by older hands when I was starting. Other growers were never reluctant to share their knowledge and experience, and I am certainly happy to pay it down the line to any new gardeners that I can help.

In-depth records and the use of different varieties is an excellent place to start extending your growing season, but other tricks can, and should, be brought into play. Two of the most effective of these are succession and relay planting.

These two techniques can be a little challenging to tell apart at first because they are so similar so let me clarify because these will be terms that you come across frequently. Relay planting is where you plant a different crop in the same space immediately after having removed the first crop. Successive planting is where you plant the same crop in a different space and at a different time, usually a few weeks after the previous one. The idea being that the first sowing ripens and can be harvested before the second sowing reaches maturity.

Both methods are designed to maximise yields by being able to use the available ground for the longest time possible. Here is where experience is really going to start to count. It is tempting to simply print down a chart from the internet or a garden manual and on the date suggested, to plug in the next crop or the next batch of seeds. Oh, if life were only that easy. The growing conditions are what will determine when the next crop can and should go in.

For example, if you want to get your spinach going really early, you plant your first early variety seeds as soon as the soil can be worked. Most charts will advise you to plant the successive crop two weeks later. That is fine in principle, but if the weather has been cold and the first sowing has not emerged from the ground, the second sowing is likely to ripen at exactly the same time, and you will have a glut of spinach that would make Pop Eye draw a sharp breath.

I wish that I could simply offer a magic formula that would overcome this but there isn't one. Though there is a successive sowing chart further into this chapter, please use it more as a guideline than a definitive process. You as the gardener will need to read the conditions in your garden and decide when the time is right to sow successive crops. It is usually preferable to have a few days between crops ripening than to have too much at any one time as this quickly gets out of hand and leads to waste.

Many of the leafy vegetables make ideal crops for succession planting.

Spinach can be sown very early using an early variety and then, by switching to later varieties will continue to give yields right up until late summer or early autumn. If this is then followed with a hardy variety over the winter months, and allowed to grow

Figure 49. Wild spinach are great for succession planting.

through a protective layer of straw, you should see a yield in early spring. That is right in the middle of the hungry gap. A similar process can be applied to kale, lettuce and broccoli.

An example of good relay plants is to start off with early potatoes and then switch to bush beans as soon as they have been lifted. If you follow a heavy feeder like corn with runner beans that trap nitrogen in the soil, you not only have a relay crop but you improve your soil at the same time.

The use of other methods can enhance both relay and succession methods. Starting seeds off in containers and then having them already established as soon as the weather is kind to you can dramatically lengthen the growing season. That method is not just restricted to the first planting of the year. Your succession crops can be grown indoors and then planted out only when the previous sowing is established. In this way, those plants growing in containers can be kept indoors for a few extra days if the weather is not to your liking.

Although starting seeds off in the house has obvious advantages, there are usually only so many windowsills that you can fill with seedlings without finding yourself in divorce court. The Rolls

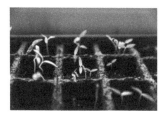

Figure 50. Starting seeds indoors.

Royce of alternatives is to have a greenhouse where you can start seedlings, shelter plants that aren't hardy, start cuttings and generally have a good time. There is no getting away from the fact that greenhouses can be an expensive investment and that will need to be weighed up in relation to the returns you can expect from your garden. We will look at greenhouse gardening later in this series, but if you have access to one or are good with your hands, then this is an investment that will definitely open up a whole new range of gardening opportunities.

Greenhouses can be heated using a variety of different methods, they are the ideal place to have built-in hotbeds, and they provide a sheltered space for the gardener to carry on working during those cold winter months.

They are, however, not totally perfect despite the heavy promotion that I have just given them. They need to be kept almost clinically clean in order not to prove a breeding ground for pests and fungal diseases, and they invariably need to be maintained because the wood-work is exposed to warm damp conditions that are so conducive to wood rot.

Even if that dream greenhouse is beyond your financial means at the moment, there are always cheaper options to consider. As a matter of fact, there can be few areas of human endeavour where cheap alternative options are explored as widely as they are in gardening. In general, we gardeners tend to be a tight-fisted bunch.

Cold frames are simple frames, generally made of timber, over which a transparent lid is fitted. This allows plants to grow in a sheltered position much like a greenhouse but for considerably less cost. My frames are made of cheap scaffold boards, and the lids are glass fridge doors that were recovered from a tip. They may not be the most attractive feature of my garden, but they have proved very useful and have been worth every penny of the two pounds that I invested in them.

Figure 51. Greenhouse filled with seed trays and plugs.

Other cold frames can be made of wood with plastic or a sheet of ordinary glass as the roof. The only thing you will need to consider is how much weight that lid can hold if it snows. Even if you don't want to shell out for a wooden frame, a sheet of glass or plastic over a frame made of blocks positioned in a square or rectangle will do the trick. A cold frame is always going to be limited by the number of plants that it can hold, but owning one can add considerably to the number of plants you can protect and thus prolong your growing season.

Cloches are glass covers that can be stood over an individual plant to help protect it from the cold. Cloche is the French word for a bell, and the French were indeed the first gardeners to use these particular items to cover plants during winter. Today, French cloches can cost a small fortune. They do look rather chic but when its minus 5°C outside and the ground is covered in mud do you really care? You can achieve the same result by cutting the top off an empty plastic drinks bottle. In fact, if you lean two sheets of glass together to form an A-frame, these will do the same job as an imported cloche. The main point to take away from this is that by providing any sort of protection through which the light can penetrate, you will help keep many plants warm enough to extend the growing season.

Tunnel farming, now often referred to as plasticulture, has so changed agriculture that in many parts of Europe we can eat crops such as tomatoes all year round. Raised beds make putting up hoops very easy and when a sheet of strong, clear plastic is attached to this, you in effect, create your tunnel. Inside that tunnel, the temperature will be several degrees warmer than outside. Very often, a few degrees can mean the difference between a seed germinating and not germinating. It also adds that bit of extra growing time that might help a plant ripen earlier or go into the bed earlier. When it comes to increasing yield and extending the growing period, something this simple could make all the difference.

We touched briefly on floating mulches earlier in this series. A floating mulch is a covering of clear plastic or light permeable fleece that is pegged down over a bed to help protect from the cold. It is cost-effective and straightforward, and even the pegs can be made from simple pieces of wire bent to make staples. When you cover a crop of any kind with a floating mulch, then always make sure that you leave enough room for the plant to grow. On warm sunny days, you can uncover the crop and then cover again before nightfall. That way, the soil will benefit from the sun's warmth and the heat will, at least partially, be trapped when the cover is pegged back in place.

Many crops are winter hardy. Garlic, for example, is planted in autumn and will then grow away quite happily during the winter and be ready to harvest early the following spring. The book on winter gardening in this series will deal with this subject in greater depth.

At the moment what I am keen for you to know is that you can grow food in your raised beds every day of the year. Lettuce, onions, kale, peas, radishes, spinach and chard are all plants that can be winter grown and which will help eliminate the hungry gap.

There are even some advantages to be gained from growing crops over the winter. There is generally very little need for water during the winter period. I switch off my irrigation system altogether during the colder months and only if it has been really dry will I give a light watering with a hose and wand. It is possible to purchase an irrigation attachment that detects when it has not rained for some time and which will then allow the water to come on. I prefer not to use this as the risk of frost damage to the irrigation system outweighs the advantages of not having to check how dry the soil is from time to time. That test simply consists of me sticking my finger into the soil to the depth of the second knuckle. If I can't feel moisture, then it is probably time for a light targeted watering.

Another significant advantage is that there are far fewer plant pests during the winter than there are at other times of the year. Even slugs and snails seem to go into hibernation, and some of the leafy crops that I harvest are the best that I will reap all year round.

The main crop harvested during winter and early spring will indeed be green leafy vegetables. If you are not a fan of these like I am, then that may seem a little disappointing. Green leafy vegetables are some of the plants most lacking in the modern diet, so you may be able to console yourself with that thought. Another is that these vegetables always seem to become more expensive during winter, so the money you save in relation to what you might have had to buy in also increases.

Figure 52. Boxed raised vegetable garden on pallet collars with fitted glass greenhouse on top.

Finally, we come to the subject of storing our harvest. In gardening terms, food storage is something of a neglected art. Gardening, after all, is all about growing things, getting dirty and wearing muddy boots. Food storage usually takes place in the kitchen and therefore is a totally different subject. If you really want to benefit from the bounty of your garden, then how you preserve what you grow is as important as gardening itself. It certainly is if you want to become as near as possible to being self- sufficient in vegetable production. Good gardeners always experience periods of feast or famine. Poor gardeners only experience the famine.

Those periods of almost glutinous productivity need to be harnessed. We can give away much of the excess in the hope that the neighbours will like us and forgive the fact that we dress badly and always seem to have dirty hands, but that won't feed us during the lean periods.

When I first started gardening, I was very uninterested when it came to preserving my produce, so I empathise with this viewpoint. I have, however, come to find preserving in all its many different forms, to be a gratifying part of the food production process. There is something profoundly rewarding about seeing row upon row of full mason jars on the pantry shelf and having a freezer brimming with beans, peas and carrots that brings out the hunter-gatherer in me. Knowing that I have enough food to live on for months and that it is all the result of my own labours provides a primitive sense of security, even if the mason jars are made of modern glass, and the freezer is powered by electricity.

If you get serious about growing your produce, then the freezer is your best friend. You will be amazed at how quickly you can fill up a big chest freezer throughout a season, and this is crucial to getting through those hungry months when the garden is less productive than it is typically.

Figure 53. Frozen homegrown wild spinach.

You can freeze most vegetables. Some people like to blanch them in boiling water first, but I don't bother and, to be honest, if your garden is in full swing, you probably won't have the time. Beans I simply wash, top and tail and then freeze as soon as they are dry. I place then in a plastic bag and squeeze out the air, and they are good to go. There is a machine that will suck the air out more thoroughly, but it really isn't necessary. Peas I shell, rinse and bag, carrots I usually slice or chop. The only thing that can really go wrong is that you fail to allow the produce to dry before freezing. All that will happen then is that they will freeze into solid chunks that are difficult to get apart when you need to cook them. Even eggplant freezes perfectly after slicing.

Most people will tell you that you cannot freeze tomatoes. This is one crop you can typically be sure of having a glut of, and because freezing is so quick and easy, I was obliged to come up with a method for doing this. I scrape out the inside of the fruit and then turn the shells upside down to drain off some of the juice. I then freeze the shells, and when I need them, I make stuffed tomatoes by merely placing my stuffing directly into the frozen shell before popping it into the oven. The inside I place in a plastic container and freeze as well. When I make the stuffed tomatoes, I defrost the inside flesh and turn it into a sauce.

For potatoes, pumpkin and squash, I chop them along with some onion and freeze them in a plastic bag. When I need to make a soup in the winter, I have one already made, and I remove the bag from the freezer and cook it in a pot with water and seasoning.

All berries, plumbs, red fruit and figs I freeze on a plastic tray. Once they are frozen, I knock them off the tray and throw them into a bag which I throw back into the freezer.

Figure 54. Frozen homegrown blueberries are perfect for refreshing milkshakes.

They will be fine for crumbles, tarts and smoothies when needed. Apples and pears, I usually freeze only after peeling and coring, but other than that, I use the same method as for other fruit. Frozen apples or pears are fine for crumbles and pies.

Bottling is my next go-to method for storing excess production. This is a little more complicated. For this to work well, you are really going to need mason jars. These you will probably have to buy, but they should pay for themselves within one season. Wash and prepare your produce and pack them into the mason jars. After that cover with salted boiling water, close and sterilise in a large pot of boiling water. Sterilising vegetables is just a matter of covering the mason jars with water in a large pot and boiling. Times vary from vegetable to vegetable, and you should check before making your preserve. If you have included meat into the preserve, then you will need to extend that sterilising time to two hours.

There are two types of mason jar. One comes with a glass lid and a rubber seal. The other comes with a two-piece metal lid. I have no particular preference, but some people swear by one or the other so you will want to experiment a little. You will need to sterilise the jars before filling, but this is just a matter of placing them in a pot of boiling water. When you are ready to add the vegetables, remove them from the boiling water, shake off most of the excess water and you are good to go.

Figure 55. Home canning of freshly picked cucumbers.

If you are using jars with the two-piece metal lid, it is a good idea to let them cool down after sterilising with the vegetable in and then unscrew the outer metal ring of the lid. The inner lid will stay in place because it has been vacuum-sealed by the heat. Dry the outer ring and replace it. This will ensure that any water that crept in does not rust the metal.

These two methods alone will enable you to preserve much of your harvest. Another method that I use when I am pressed for time is the ratatouille method. I fry up onions, garlic, peppers, eggplant, courgettes and tomatoes and season well. For good measure, I might toss in some black olives. Once cooked this mixture can be either frozen or preserved in mason jars. All I then need to do is warm it up when needed, and it is an ideal way to store large quantities of vegetables all at once. Over a day, I might make enough ratatouille to last for a year, and it is a profoundly comforting feeling seeing all those ready-cooked meals lining up the shelves of the pantry.

Figure 56. There is something somehow magical about homemade jams, marmalades and preserves.

Jam is another storage method that is very easy and which will prolong the life of your harvest. Don't think this only applies to fruit. Pumpkin, tomatoes and squash can all be turned into jams, either combined with fruit or on their own. Once you start delving into the exotic art of jam, making you will be amazed at the broad spectrum of recipes available.

Here you don't need to go the expense of buying bottles. Simply collect jars from supermarket purchases or ask you less self-sufficient friends to do so. Boil both the jars and the lids in boiling water for ten minutes. Once your jam is ready, remove the jars from the water but not the lids. Place the hot jam into the jars, remove the lids from the hot water and fit them immediately, then turn the bottles upside down to cool. You can store that jam for years.

Other vegetables will store for months without needing to go to such lengths as boiling or freezing. Pumpkins kept in a cool dark place have a very long shelf life. To extend this, stand them on some straw and always make sure not to bruise them during the harvesting process. Carrots can be plunged into dry sand with just the green tops sticking out. These too will last right through the winter. Many varieties of apple can be wrapped in newspaper and stored on a shelf in a cellar or cool dark cupboard. Don't let them touch one another, and their shelf life will carry them well into winter.

Garlic and onions can last a long time if they are kept dry though both of them can be pickled in vinegar, which means they can be kept virtually indefinitely. Many vegetables lend themselves to pickling including cucumbers, onions, mushrooms and cabbage. Cabbage is also made into sauerkraut, and that subject has become so popular in recent years that it has become almost a cult movement.

Fruits such as raspberries, strawberries, red currants and melons can also be preserved in syrup or alcohol. All of these methods not only prolong the life of your produce, but they also add variety and colour to your diet. None of these are tasks that you will master overnight. Instead, they tend to be learned over time and in accordance with where the most abundance occurs in the crop yield. With each new method mastered, the less of a threat the hungry season becomes. Eventually, you reach a point that your preserved stocks are so large that they will not only carry you through the season immediately ahead but possibly even the season after that. Suddenly, self-sufficiency in both fruit and vegetables no longer seems just a romantic notion.

6

ADVANCED SOIL ENRICHMENT

W hilst crop management will always be important; it will never reach its true potential unless it is riding on a foundation of good soil management. It is vital to grasp that soil stewardship lies at the heart of all good gardening. Right from the start of this series, we have tried to instil that a gardener's crop can only be as good as the growing medium that goes into those raised beds. In this chapter, we will try to build on that foundation, because it is here that so many gardeners stumble.

When you first started your raised beds, you may well have been so keen to get planting that you took some shortcuts at the soil preparation stage. I know that I did. I purchased soil from someone that may have held his wallet in higher regard than he did my future garden production. He was a swimming pool maker, and he was as eager to sell me topsoil as I was to buy it. The net result was that much of the soil I bought might not have been topsoil. Instead of a healthy life-giving base filled with living organisms, what I ended up purchasing was more of a desert wasteland. I was just too inexperienced to recognise this at the time. There was enough zest in that soil to give me a good first crop, but after that, the decline was so noticeable that even in my eagerness, I was forced to recognise that I had been somewhat had.

As it turned out, the experience I gained from revitalising the soil and bringing it back to full health has served me well, and so it became just another one of life's little lessons. It could easily have caused a new gardener to decide he lacked the green fingers required to garden successfully and so give up altogether becoming just another supermarket supporter.

Figure 57. A good garden starts with a good soil.

What I came away with, and what I hope you too will learn from my misfortune, is that soil can be transformed. It is a substance that is almost eager to resume its role as a material that can sustain life. Providing what you have put into your beds is not actually toxic waste from some nuclear plant, there is a good chance that with a little tender care and patience, you can bring it back to health.

No matter how good soil is, regardless of whether it is encased in a raised bed or you are planting into open ground, the soil will become degraded simply through having nutrients drawn from it by successive crops. When man first began the transition, from hunter-gatherer to farmer, he did not understand this and as a result, was forced to move on every few seasons as the soil became degraded or too heavily populated by pests or diseases. We see the same thing happening in the amazon where forests are burned down and planted but where the soil will only sustain crops for one or two seasons. If those farmers had a better under-standing of good soil stewardship, then we might not find ourselves in a place where hundreds of thousands of acres of forest were being burned each year.

Raised beds are basically containers, and a gardener can simply replace the soil inside of them every few years, though at some cost in terms of both labour and finance. With good soil management, the need to change the soil is eliminated. Instead, an ongoing refreshment takes place that is far less costly and much more environmentally sustainable. If this sounds like it might be complicated, then look at the forest as an example. With no added nutrients, the forest manages to sustain some of the largest plants on earth. It does this by continually revitalising the soil with dead plant material in an ongoing process that never stops. Those massive and healthy trees do not need chemical fertilisers or fancy enrichment systems, and yet they thrive.

COMPOST: PROTEIN POWDER FOR YOUR GARDEN

My first choice for bringing soil to optimal health is compost. As you will have gathered as you have read through these books, I am a great believer in compost. It is, in my opinion, the bodybuilding tonic that every garden needs to reach optimal performance. It is natural, easy to produce and free. What is more, is that it is made from materials that would generally go to waste. It is a perfectly balanced nutrient supply, a soil conditioner, a mulch, and it helps retain moisture. How much more can you ask of a free product than that?

Over recent years compost has gone through some-thing of a renaissance as gardeners, businesses and individuals have woken up to its potential. In part, this has been fuelled by the green movement as they have fought to encourage people to move away from synthetic chemical fertilisers and rediscover this wonder material that has always been at our fingertips. I say rediscover because compost is one thing that gardeners have been using effectively for millennia. The widespread use of chemical substitutes really only gained traction after World War II.

Figure 58. It is not only dead easy to make but also costs nothing.

Because compost promotes microbial balance, it does not just feed the plants, but the whole mini-ecosystem that exists in healthy soil. A well-balanced soil becomes a sort of living organism in its own right.

The most significant disadvantage of compost is time. Because it is a naturally occurring material, it takes time to make and time for the nutrients and microorganisms to build up to create a balanced soil environment the gardener so desires.

Man has become incredibly impatient recently, and this is a trait that fell straight into the hands of the synthetic fertiliser industry. Why wait for your soil to develop when with one quick application, you can supply the exact nutrients that the plants were lacking. This argument was incredibly powerful when sold to the agricultural industry. They had been practising monoculture on an ever-increasing scale, and this was a sure-fire way to denude soils of specific nutrients. Fertilisers overcame that deficiency in one fell swoop.

The problem with the quick fix solution is that it created a cycle of dependency. Each year fertiliser would be added to the soil to replace that absorbed by the crop, and each year the natural soil ecosystem would be depleted. To add to the problem, whilst it was possible to ensure that enough chemicals were supplied to meet the needs of the plants, it was challenging to know whether too much was being applied and what was happening to the excess. We now know that excess fertiliser use is having a catastrophic effect on the environment.

With nitrogen products alone, we pour 120 million tons onto our fields each year and half of that leaches into rivers and from there makes its way to the ocean. What this results in is algal growth which creates dead zones which cannot support life. This is not some small-scale issue either. Last year the dead zone in the Gulf of Mexico reached 8,800 square miles in size. I don't know about you, but I don't want to participate in the production of toxic tides and dead rivers; especially when there is a far healthier alternative available right on my doorstep if I exhibit just a little bit of patience.

Clearly, I am starting to rant here, and rather than keep going until I foam at the mouth, something I could easily do when talking about this subject, why not look at some ways to get your compost production started.

There are many ways to make compost and some are quicker than others. For reasons I don't quite understand, some people have made composting into this hugely complicated procedure that can leave you feeling like you need a degree in chemistry just to produce a few buckets full. What I am going to propose is a far more simple method that has served me perfectly well for years as it did my grandparents before me.

To make good compost, you need four things. Green waste, brown waste, moisture and air. Green waste is derived mainly from plant materials such as grass clippings, household food scraps, prunings and weeds. Brown waste is woodier and can be from cardboard, non-glossy paper, sawdust, dried leaves or woody material. Green waste is high in nitrogen which is the most essential nutrient in plant growth, and brown waste contains carbon.

To speed up the breakdown process, most brown material should be shredded or cut up finely with secateurs. What you are trying to achieve is a dark, crumbly material that is full of microbes and rich in garden worms. This is where compost purists often get into a heated debate. What percentage of green waste should you incorporate to your mix and what percentage of brown? To be honest with you, I don't have the time to sit around, weighing my waste materials and estimating percentages. When I have lawn clippings, they go in, when I have hedge clippings, they go in. If I can score a pile of old bedding straw from the neighbouring farmer, so much the better. I am reasonably sure that I end up with an overall percentage that is around fifty-fifty, but that may be out on any given day, according to what waste I have collected. Some people suggest a fifty-fifty mix; others recommend a one part green waste to three parts brown. How they get any gardening done when they are so focused on these minutiae of composting is beyond me.

If you have too much green waste, the compost will tell you by going sludgy and starting to smell bitter. Too much brown and the breakdown process will grind to a halt. Don't stress about either event. Just add more of whatever ingredient is lacking and the whole heap will soon self-regulate.

Figure 59. Good organic compost.

The secret to good compost lies in regular turning as this is what adds the air. The more often you turn the heap, the more oxygen it will contain and the more the microbe level will build-up, which in turn will speed the breakdown process. Turning a large compost heap is physical work. I happen to like physical exercise, and my compost making activities have saved me a small fortune in gym fees over the years. If you prefer to take a less physical approach, then make your compost in a large bin and when the bin is full just kick it over and leave the contents on the ground. The air will have been allowed in, and the composting process will continue.

Good compost gets hot. It can easily reach an internal temperature of around 60° Celsius. If your compost is steaming, it is a good sign. It tells you that microbial activity is operating a maximum potential. The less heat, the slower the process, but if you pile green and brown waste together, it will compost eventually, heat or no heat.

You will hear a whole list of things that you should not add to your compost heap. These include newspaper, citrus, eggshells, garden weeds and cooked food. There are various theories behind this advice, but I ignore all of them. Get your microbe level up to the right levels, and your compost heap will digest anything. There is a very well-known YouTube gardener who buried dead chickens and even a dead kangaroo in his garden, within a matter of months, the microbes had broken those carcasses down to the point where they were additional nutrition for the plants.

While I don't advocate scouring the countryside for roadkill or other carcasses, it does prove my point that a compost heap will eventually digest just about anything apart from old cars. Think of your heap as a giant hungry creature living in the bottom of the garden with broad dietary tastes and an indestructible digestive system.

The only things that don't go into my compost are cat, dog or human faeces, and meat or dairy waste. All of these products would, I am sure, would eventually breakdown. I will, however, be handling the compost and even I need to draw the line occasionally. I have done a tour on an industrial compost facility that deals successfully with hotel waste that includes meat and bones on an ongoing basis, and it is possible to buy pelleted human waste as a fertiliser, but I haven't quite reached that point yet. Clippings from evergreens such as Leylandii just take too long to compost, and so does the moss that I rake from my lawn. These go onto the bonfire, and the ash from that later makes its way onto the heap.

I know my cavalier approach will shock those who have spent years advocating a far stricter approach to compost management, but the fact of the matter is that what I do works. There are easy methods to ensure that your compost is progressing well. The first is to smell it. Compost has a sweet smell similar to what you might notice on the floor of a forest. If it smells bitter or like it is fermenting then chances are you have the ratio of green to brown waste too high. Add more brown material, and the situation will soon correct itself, especially if you turn the material in and allow some air to penetrate.

Moisture control will vary greatly depending on what your weather conditions are. If you live in an area with plenty of rain, then you can reduce the water intake by throwing an old carpet over your compost. If you experience dry spells, then you may need to water lightly from time to time. To test for the correct moisture level, simply pick up a handful of compost and squeeze it tightly. No water should drip out of it, and when you open your hand, the compost should have bound together. Heat is another tell-tale sign that things are progressing well, but the real indicator is the presence of earthworms. Turn over a spade full of healthy compost, and it will be teeming with these creatures.

The composting debate continues just as hotly when you delve into what container you should keep your compost in. There is a wide range of options, and they vary from free to very expensive. There are pros and cons to all of them and they all work.

144 | ADVANCED RAISED BED GARDENING GUIDE

I use a straightforward three-bay system made out of reclaimed pallets. I hammer posts into the ground as support to create a three-walled container using three pallets. Next to that, I add two more containers, but these only need two pallets each as they share a wall of the adjoining container. This leaves me with three containers of about one cubic meter each. I like to start my compost directly on the ground, so I don't lay anything over the base. That earth is, after all, full of healthy microbes that will soon make their way up into my compost.

Once the first container is about half full of a mixture of green and brown waste, I toss it over into the second container and then start filling the first one again. This airs the compost that I began with.

I do the same thing with the second load of compost. As soon as the container is half-filled, I toss it into the second container where it joins the oldest compost. In theory that second container should now be full, but you will be amazed how much the breaking down process reduces the size of the pile. I can do a third and sometimes even a fourth transfer before that middle container is full. When it is, I toss it into the third container. This gives it more air and the compost is now virtually ready to use but can continue sitting there until I am ready for it. In the meantime, container one is steadily filling again, and the whole process has become an ongoing chain production of raw materials in at one end and compost out at the other.

The speed of the filling process varies depending on the time of year and whether I manage to entice any animal bedding out of my neighbours. There is also no strict rule as to how fast the process will take as this is dependent on the materials going in, the weather and how often I turn the mix. Most people suggest that six months is the minimum, but I believe that time can be considerably reduced if you turn the mix regularly. As the compost gets healthier and hotter, it starts to convert new material more quickly.

Figure 60. A three bay compost system.

Of course, you don't need to use my Scrooge-like pallet system. Compost can be made in plastic bins, containers made from ply or galvanised iron or they can be bought purpose-made. It is possible to buy bins that are suspended on a frame and can be turned by simply winding a handle. Whilst this works effectively, for more extensive gardens, it might be too small, and you would then need a series of them to meet the garden's needs. You also don't necessarily need any container and can make a large pile of green and brown layered material that will produce perfectly good compost providing you turn it from time to time. Even if you live in an apartment, you can keep a small bin on the kitchen counter to gather household scraps and then transfer it to a larger bin on the balcony every day or two.

In short, composting is a very natural and straight forward process which can save you a considerable amount of money, benefits the environment, and it will transform the productivity of your raised beds. Don't be put off by people who try to overcomplicate this age-old method. Humans have been composting since long before the study of percentages or the advent of the tumbler bin.

Generally, I try to always be at a point where I have at least one container of garden compost that is ready and can be added to my beds as and when it is needed. When I plant a crop, I mulch with compost, when I lift a crop, I dig some compost into the bed as soon as the crop comes out. If I haven't planted a cover crop and the bed is going to be empty over winter, then I cover it in a layer of compost. Suppose the soil in my beds is looking low then I bulk them up with compost. In short, I am continually reinvigorating my soil with compost as often as is feasible.

Figure 61. Ecology waste.

LASAGNA GARDENING:

Many gardeners use this system when they start their beds, and it is also sometimes called the layering system. It operates in much the same way as making compost does. They start with an inch or two of brown material followed by an inch or two of green waste and build those layers up one after the other until they have filled their beds. They finish with a layer of brown waste that acts as a blanket until the contents of the bed have broken down and are ready to plant. This process of breaking down takes around six months, and you can tell when it is complete because none of the original green or brown material that went into the bed will be recognisable once breakdown is complete.

The depths of the bed don't need to have all broken down as long as the top few inches are sufficiently composted to plant into. In this way, what you are actually doing is making compost but in a raised bed. I prefer to have my compost where I can apply it as and when I need it, but that is down to personal choice. Personally, I don't like a bed to be out of action for months while the breakdown is happening. If I make the mix directly in the bed, I can't turn it and speed the procedure. I also always like to include natural soil as this always contains those microorganisms that are so essential to the speed of the breakdown process. If you go down the lasagna route, then be prepared for the fact that the contents of the bed will shrink dramatically. You can compensate for this by overfilling the bed by quite a large margin.

If I am not applying a cover crop, and the bed is not going to be planted over the winter months, I may apply compost that has not fully broken down as this can take place in the beds and will free up space in my compost bins at the same time. I think this also further demonstrates how much composting and lasagna gardening have in common. They are more or less the same thing but done in different parts of the garden.

OTHER SOIL ADDITIVES.

Compost is cheap and practical, but depending on your situation, you may have access to other products that you can use that will do a similar job or can be used in conjunction with compost.

SPENT MUSHROOM COMPOST:

There used to be a time when if you lived near a mushroom farm, you could get hold of their waste product for free. Mushroom farmers have become a little savvier to what scroungers gardeners can be, and you may end up having to pay for this product now, though it shouldn't be costly. If you do happen to live near a mushroom farm, it is still worth hitching up your trailer and going down there in some worn clothes looking poor and needy. You could well come away with your trailer filled for free. Don't forget to drop off a box full of vegetables at the end of the season to keep the system oiled.

Mushroom compost is usually made from chicken or horse manure mixed with straw or hay and then steam sterilised. The mushrooms are fungi, and they feed on a whole different range of nutrients to vegetables, so the compost that is being disposed of is still brimming with goodness for the gardener and is a wonderful soil conditioner which provides both permeability and aeration qualities.

Ideally, the compost should have aged for a while before you apply it to your beds, but this process has often already taken place at the mushroom farm where it may well have been laying around for months. It can raise the soil alkaline level and so may not be ideal for cane fruits. On the other hand, it will be appreciated by brassicas such as cabbage, kale, broccoli and Brussel sprouts and may decrease the risk of clubroot disease. Early spring is an excellent time to include this product into your beds.

COFFEE GRINDS:

Coffee shops have begun to pop up on every high street over the last two decades, and each of them produces an incredible amount of vegetable waste in the form of coffee grinds. Despite its brown colouring, this waste product should be regarded as green waste rather than brown carbon waste. Most coffee shops will be happy to give it away as there seems to be no commercial value to it at this stage. The problem you will encounter is not so much that they don't want to give it to you, but instead, they don't want to store it while waiting for you to be in a position to collect it. You will need to negotiate a deal whereby you collect it regularly or supply them with some sort of large bin in which they can put it aside.

Figure 62. Coffee grinds used as fertilisers.

Coffee grinds come with all sorts of myths attached to them. Some suggest that they are a deterrent to slugs and snails, but tests have shown this not to be the case. Others claim they are detrimental to plants but that is also not true. The most significant risk they pose when used in the raised bed is that they are very fine and therefore, can act a bit like clay in that they bind together. This has the potential to cause water drainage problems. I have never found this to be an issue. Once I have spread a layer across the surface of the bed, I simply rake it into the soil lightly, and that combines it enough that the binding issue ceases to occur. If I manage to get hold of substantial quantities, I add it to the compost heap and let the worms do the mixing. The grinds appear to have no adverse effect on the worms, and I have found no studies that suggest they may have trouble sleeping at night due to the boost in caffeine intake.

FARMYARD MANURE:

Farmyard manure is a precious resource if you can get hold of it. Contrary to popular city perceptions, manure does not smell bad as long as it has had a few months to break down. Ideally, you want it to arrive when it has already had some time to do this, but it is such a valuable resource that you should take it in whatever state you can get hold of it. If there is still a smell to it, then cover it with soil or compost and let it sit for a few months.

Fresh manure is too strong to apply to beds that are going to have crops in them in the near future. It is easily capable of burning their roots. If the manure you receive is fresh then you can

Figure 63. Farmyard and animal manures.

layer it into a bed using the layering method and, in a few months, it will have broken down sufficiently to be planted. It provides a high nutrient source as well as improving moisture retention. If you don't have a bed that you want out of action for the months that it will take to break down the manure then simply feed it gradually into the compost heap. You can even simply ignore it for a few months and then apply it to the beds as a top dressing once it has broken down.

GREEN WASTE:

The combination of garden and kitchen will almost inevitably generate large amounts of green waste. It is easy enough to use this on the compost, but it can also go directly into your beds. Kitchen waste, hedge clippings and lawn clippings can all be layered into the bed where they will break down over time. You don't want to do this in beds that are currently planted but rather into beds that will be dormant for a few months so that the breakdown process will have time to take place. When I harvest things such as cabbages or broccoli, I cut them off at soil level and leave the roots to break down where they will add to the health of the soil.

Provided your top twelve inches of soil is already broken down, it is possible to have deeper layers that are still undergoing this process and still plant on top of them. I never find this a very practical approach other than when filling a bed for the first time. Generally, I prefer to add green waste to the compost heap and then use the composted material either

Figure 64. Fruit waste helping the compost heap decompose more efficiently.

as a soil ameliorant or a top dressing. All of that green waste is moisture retentive and serves to build up the microbiome upon which your plants will thrive. There are a few materials such as clippings of Leylandii and moss that take so long to break down that they should not be added to either beds or compost. Weeds, on the other hand, compost perfectly well and, unless they have gone to seed, any weeds I pull out between the rows of plants I will simply leave on the soil surface to breakdown.

ALTERNATIVE NITROGEN SOURCES:

There is any number of other sources of nitrogen that can be added to the raised bed and many of these can be purchased at garden centres where they usually come in bags. These include alfalfa pellets, soybean meal and even pelleted human waste. They can be mixed into the beds, and they will soon break down and become part of the natural feeding system. I always manage to generate or scrounge so much material that I never seem to need to go to the expense of buying in these additives, but you made need to consider them if you are just starting and your garden had not yet started to create enough green material.

CARBON MATERIAL:

As with green waste, brown waste can also be purchased in any number of different forms. These include coir and peat. Sawdust, straw wood chips and even torn up cardboard will do almost the same thing. All of them are high in carbon and are good at retaining moisture which is their primary function.

Leaf mould is one free resource that I believe is hugely undervalued. If you have even just one or two deciduous trees in your garden then, come autumn, you are going to have an abundance of dry leaves and so often people simply burn this excellent carbon source. Indeed, dry leaves are not high in nutrients, but that does not mean they are without merit. Once broken down, leaf mould is a near-perfect soil conditioner, and it has terrific moisture retention capabilities.

I gather my fallen leaves in cages made from chicken wire. There is really nothing sophisticated about these. They consist of four posts driven into the ground with chicken wire attached. Their primary function is to stop the leaves blowing away before they start to break down. Once they have broken down a little and become damp, then their own weight stops them blowing about and they can just be stored in a heap. Most people will tell you that it takes two years to make usable leaf mould, but I always do it in half that time, and the reason for this is that I add a sprinkling of blood meal from time to time and I turn the material regularly. That dramatically speeds up the breakdown process. By the time the first leaves are falling in autumn, the previous year's material has become black and crumbly. I can add it to my beds, use it as a mulch or simply boost my compost with it. If It took two years to get to a usable state, then I would need twice as many cages.

Using my system, the cages I have are empty just in time to fill with the next leaf fall.

IMPROVING DRAINAGE:

So far, all the materials we have looked at have been aimed primarily at increasing moisture retention and adding or replacing nutrients. There may be occasions where you are more interested in increasing the drainage of your beds because they are retaining too much moisture. If you have created a healthy growing medium, this should be quite rare, and you may need to first look at other reasons that the beds are becoming boggy. It could be that the beds are sitting on a material such as clay that is not allowing water to escape or it could be that the sides of the bed are holding the water in too much. Both of these instances are physical factors rather than being a problem related to the growing medium itself. If that is the case, you may need to dig drainage trenches or even drill holes into the sides of the beds.

If the growing medium you have created is high in clay, then drainage might be slow, and you may need to do something about it. Usually, this is rare because as the clay is combined with other green and brown layers, it naturally loses its binding capacity and becomes more free draining. You can hurry this up a bit by mixing sharp sand into the soil. The larger sand granules open up spaces within the clay and over time drainage will be improved. It is a good idea to wash the sand before mixing it into the soil. Both sea sand and building sand can contain minerals that can be harmful to plants.

The other alternative is to purchase vermiculite which is a material made from crushed organic rock. It is chemically neutral and is very good at assisting drainage. It can be purchased at most garden centres but is generally intended for use as an additive to potting soil. On a large scale such as a raised bed garden, it can be quite an expensive way of solving a water retention issue.

COAL DUST:

Another soil intervention that you still sometimes hear of is the addition of coal soot or crushed charcoal to the surface of the soil. This idea dates back many years to a time when Victorian gardeners applied these materials to their beds to cause them to heat up a little earlier in the season. This was mainly done in areas where winters were long and summers were short. The black dust would trap heat, and a few extra degrees could be gained, thus prolonging the growing season.

You still hear of this method being used from time to time, but the advent of black plastic sheeting has almost entirely wiped it out. If you live in an area where winters seem to go on forever, you could cover the surface of your beds with black plastic sheeting. Providing it is tucked in well it will trap heat, and the ground will become workable slightly earlier. A better result might be obtained by applying a thick mulch of dark compost though if there was a great deal of rain, the heat retentive benefits might be offset by the water.

COVER CROPS:

Cover crops are another easy and effective way to keep your beds in pristine health. They are easy to grow and offer many advantages. They suppress weeds, increase organic matter, recycle soil nutrients and retain moisture, so there is little not to like about them. The only reason I can see for not using cover crops is that you are going to grow vegetables all year round.

All year production is a great aspiration, but many people simply don't want to be gardening in the cold and wet, especially if they don't get back from their day job until after dark. Even if you do manage to keep most of your garden in full-time production, there are probably going to be one or two beds sitting idle and here is where cover crops can be of great benefit.

There are hundreds of cover crops to choose from, but they fall into two main categories. Legumes include plants such as vetch, soybeans, clover and peas. It is important to understand that you are not growing them for harvest but as a cover crop. You will not be allowing them to reach full crop bearing maturity. This family of crops are nitrogen binding, so they are reinforcing the nutrient level of your soil.

The second group are grain crops such as rye, oats and wheat. Although they don't have the same nitrogen binding capacity, they break down easily and therefore can be readily dug back into the soil when they are cut back.

Most cover crops grow quickly. Spread the seed of your chosen crop evenly and then rake the soil lightly and water in. If you still have a crop in the ground, like cabbages, for example, you can get the seeds started and have the cabbages harvested before the cover crop is at a size which will impede the cabbage.

The important thing with most cover crops is not to let them set seed; otherwise, you will have to deal with self-set seedlings popping up amongst your crop the following season. The best and most effective way of avoiding this is to cut the crop down as it starts to flower. This also happens to be the time when the plant is most loaded with nutrients which you will now be returning to the soil. You can mow the crop down with a lawnmower or strimmer, cut it down with hedge clippers or dig it over with a fork. The fallen plant material can then either be dug into the bed or simply left lying on the surface where it will break down naturally. Whichever method you opt for, expect about two months for the plant material to break down to a point where the bed is ready for planting.

Figure 65. Healthy soil.

All of these methods are good for maintaining the structure, microbial life and water retentive capacity of your soil. Although feeding with liquid organic fertilizers such as nettle tea and some of the others we have mentioned, there is nothing that can quite match an overall healthy soil. I urge you to get used to the feel texture and smell of this life-supporting product. It will enable you to become better at recognizing what healthy soil should look like, and you will soon reach a point where you can identify soil deficiencies almost instinctively. It really is the life force behind all gardening endeavours.

CONCLUSION

When you first started to consider the concept of growing vegetables in raised beds, the idea may have seemed a little counter-intuitive. We have, after all, been growing our crops directly in the ground since time immemorial. I hope now that you have been persuaded that this technique is not only practical but that it also offers many advantages.

In many ways, it differs little from more traditional methods of growing vegetables except that it takes some of the backaches out of work and allows for greater control of the growing medium. We might not have reached a point where this system is practical on a large-scale commercial basis. Still, for the small producer, particularly one with limited space available, it offers many plusses.

One added advantage is that raised beds can, when well designed, be aesthetically pleasing. While the large-scale farmer probably doesn't really care about this, if you are living in an urban environment, then why not have the benefits of something that pleases the eye as well as stocks the larder. Your neighbours will probably appreciate it too.

Figure 66. Rhubarb in a local farm raised garden.

Raised beds can produce almost all of the crops that can be grown in the ground and often with better yields. The beds themselves can be as complicated or as simple as you the gardener chooses to make them. I suspect that if you follow a similar path to the one that I did, your designs and use of materials will develop as you gain in both confidence and experience. The same thing applies to your choice of plants. In the first book in this series, we stuck to those plants that are most commonly consumed. In this book, we have taken a more comprehensive look at vegetables and fruit, but we have still to scratch the tip of the iceberg. A gardener only needs to glance through a plant catalogue to understand that the pallet of vegetables we are accustomed to eating is minute when compared to what is out there. More and more frequently, we are offered seeds from Asia, Africa and South America, and they are opening up a whole new range of products for us to grow and eat.

Above all, I have tried to convey my belief that we can garden sustainably without seeing massive drops in yield due to pests or nutrient deficiencies. The organic movement is starting to gather momentum. At this stage, we have still to see that spreading into the more massive corporate farming arena, but it is undeniably happening among small producers. They are being rewarded by a buying public keen to purchase food that they know is both healthy for their families and sustainable for the planet. If you are starting to ride this wave, then I believe that your timing is right because it is a trend that is showing no sign of diminishing.

The emphasis of the first two books in this series, and those to follow, will always be on sustainability simply because I believe that all of the evidence points towards its importance, not just in the long term but also in the years that lie just ahead. Once the bug for growing your own food bites, then you will soon want to be sure that what you are offering your family and friends is of the best quality possible. If it is contaminated by chemicals you don't really understand, then you will always wonder if what you produce is healthy. There have been so many scandals related to the big agrochemical companies in recent years that it is difficult to distinguish fact from fiction. All I do know is that if I pay the proper attention to my soil, then I don't need them. I can produce healthy, chemical-free, environmentally friendly vegetables without needing to trust what it says on the side of a bottle of pesticide or bag of fertilizer. What is more, now that you have read this book, so can you.

Throughout this series of books, you will see that sustainability lies at the heart of all my gardening techniques. I make no apology for that. You will also discover that nearly all of the techniques link into each other at some point. That is not through some master plan on my part. It is derived from the fact that gardening is a natural and integrated process and many of the subjects overlap and build on one another. In the next book on companion planting, you will see that soil quality and choice of plants remains as crucial as it was in the first two books.

Figure 67. Ecology and homegrown concept in a wooden raised garden bed.

Thank you for reading my book. If you have enjoyed reading it perhaps you would like to leave a star rating and a review for me on Amazon? It really helps support writers like myself create more books. You can leave a review for me by scanning the QR code below:

Thank you so much.

Peter Shepperd

REFERENCES

Figure 1. Mai U. (2015). Garden raised bed Khol. [photograph]. *Pixabay.*

https://pixabay.com/photos/garden-raised-bed-kohl-gardening-883095/

Figure 2. Fewings N. (2020). A colourful selection of Winter vegetables, locally produced and sourced. [photograph]. *Unsplash.*

https://unsplash.com/photos/O6ZhaRtXa3Q

Figure 3. Caniceus J. (2020). Garden vegetables cultivation. [photograph]. *Pixabay.*

https://pixabay.com/photos/garden-vegetables-cultivation-5440798/

Figure 4. Helbig A. Lehmhof Lindig - recognized recreation center with Barnyard Cafe, ecological building, clay therapy, herbal Terrace, Raised Bed, Garden Kitchen and holiday apartments. [photograph]. *Shutterstock.*

https://www.shutterstock.com/image-photo/lehmhof-lindig-recognized-recreation-center-barnyard-386661694

Figure 5. Subiyanto K. (2020). Laptop and document on table in garden. [photograph]. *Pexel.*

https://www.pexels.com/photo/laptop-and-documents-on-table-in-garden-4559532/

Figure 6. Vaivirga. Strawberries grows up in raised garden bed. Pyramid raised garden. [photograph]. *Shutterstock.*

https://www.shutterstock.com/image-photo/strawberries-grows-raised-garden-bed-pyramid-749987719

Figure 7. Sincerely Media. (2020). Green plants on brown wooden crates. [photograph]. *Unsplash.*

https://unsplash.com/photos/Agr1YTrzYPI

Figure 8. Julitt. Ripe garden strawberries grow on raised beds made of concrete in a private household. [photograph]. *Shutterstock.*

https://www.shutterstock.com/image-photo/ripe-garden-strawberries-grow-on-raised-1889112070

Figure 9. Morrissy B. (2020). Brown hay roll on green grass field during day time. [photograph]. *Unsplash.*

https://unsplash.com/photos/Pyhu5UboB10

Figure 10. Syricova T. (2020). Little girl carrying wooden log. [photograph]. *Pexels.*

https://www.pexels.com/photo/little-girl-carrying-wooden-log-3849945/

Figure 11. Shevtsova D. (2020). Person Holding Green Vegetables. [photograph]. *Pexels.*

https://www.pexels.com/photo/person-holding-green-vegetables-3629537/

Figure 12. Sailer J. (2019). Brown hay on grass. [photograph]. *Unsplash.*

https://unsplash.com/photos/EyktFS6xeQw

Figure 13. Arns N. (2018). Green leafed plant. [photograph]. *Unsplash.*

https://unsplash.com/photos/VMNmf0aARuQ

Figure 14. Sincerely Media. (2020). Green plants on white wooden crates. [photograph]. Unsplash.

https://unsplash.com/photos/uLFxO9bkVs8

Figure 15. Aldana A. (2017). Vegetal. [photograph]. *Unsplash.*

https://unsplash.com/photos/HfH5yd70ox8

Figure 16. Planet_fox. (2020). Garden salad raised bed. [photograph]. *Pixabay.*

https://pixabay.com/photos/garden-salad-raised-bed-nutrition-5223912/

Figure 17. Saentep A. Agriculture planted with secretive film to prevent weeds.organic farming.No use chemicals for good food, health , and world conservation. [photograph]. *Shutterstock.*

https://www.shutterstock.com/image-photo/agriculture-planted-secretive-film-prevent-weeds-1165972468

Figure 18. Henderson M. (2019). Backyard, Vega restaurant Rotterdam. [photograph]. *Unsplash.*

https://unsplash.com/photos/sCl3th_80_M

Figure 19. Czerwinski P. (2018). I'm not a fan of shopping malls and the one in the photo is probably the newest in Wrocław. Anyway, I looked at the building from all the sides and I found this wall to be the most interesting. [photograph]. *Unsplash.*

https://unsplash.com/photos/It65_5HA-I4

Figure 20. AltEsc Photography. (2020). Freshly plucked form farm, sun kissed vegetables in hues of green, yellow and earthy. [photograph]. *Unsplash.*

https://unsplash.com/photos/R_n3WU2sh70

Figure 21. Leone U. (2018). Celery plant. [photograph]. *Pixabay.*

https://pixabay.com/photos/celery-plant-celery-plant-3654966/

Figure 22. Paduret D.C. (2020). Black fruit on green leaves during daytime. [photograph]. *Unsplash.*

https://unsplash.com/photos/8cqlBGw84oU

Figure 23. Kovaleva P. (2020). Purple onion on white textile. [photograph]. *Pexels.*

https://www.pexels.com/photo/purple-onion-on-white-textile-5644866/

Figure 24. Ganaj P. (2020). Bright beetle on green plant in countryside. [photograph]. *Pexels.*

https://www.pexels.com/photo/bright-beetle-on-green-plant-in-countryside-4112215/

Figure 25. Kamelev E. (2017). Close-up Photography of Red Spider Mites. [photograph]. *Pexels.*

https://www.pexels.com/photo/close-up-photography-of-red-spider-mites-760223/

Figure 26. Kamelev E. (2018). Beetle On Green Leaf In Close-up Photography. [photograph]. *Pexels.*

https://www.pexels.com/photo/beetle-on-green-leaf-in-close-up-photography-1126777/

Figure 27. Shmidt J. (2017). Fresh from the garden, a beautiful perfect cauliflower. [photograph]. *Unsplash.*

https://unsplash.com/photos/0XVrBLy73rw

Figure 28. Tkaczuk J. Violet cabbage plants in the veggie garden under netting mesh - protection from pest without using pesticides. [photograph]. *Shutterstock.*

https://www.shutterstock.com/image-photo/violet-cabbage-plants-veggie-garden-under-1905743251

Figure 28. Lauria J. (2021). Cute caterpillar on a stick. [photograph]. *Unsplash.*

https://unsplash.com/photos/XtsVCzURcaE

Figure 30. Siracusa C. (2017). As a food blogger, I spend a lot of time photographing cooked dishes. But lately I've been drawn to raw ingredients in their natural state. I just fell in love with these artichokes in the market one day and even though I didn't need them for a recipe and even though they were a little pricey, I was moved to try and capture their story. To me, they seem so confident in their beauty, imperfect as it is. And so calm and peaceful in this rustic setting. [photograph]. *Unsplash.*

https://unsplash.com/photos/ErMaQGihZvI

Figure 31. Waheed J. (2018). Raw parsnips. [photograph]. *Unsplash.*

https://unsplash.com/photos/Bt-T8tSfBkM

Figure 32. Bohm A. (2018). Potatoes harvest autumn. [photograph]. *Pixabay.*

https://pixabay.com/photos/potatoes-harvest-autumn-color-3783878/

Figure 33. Shin C.M. (2016). Sweet potatoes garden plot. [photograph]. *Pixabay.*

https://pixabay.com/photos/sweet-potato-garden-plot-thu-harvest-1241696/

Figure 34. Hughes E. (2018). Nature sweet potato grow. [photograph]. *Pixabay.*

https://pixabay.com/photos/nature-sweet-potato-grow-vegetable-3364949/

Figure 35. Klein D. (2019). Yellow corn photo. [photograph]. *Unsplash.*

https://unsplash.com/photos/aglLffkAPxc

Figure 36. Volkovski K. (2019). Green corn plant. [photograph]. *Unsplash.*

https://unsplash.com/photos/Q_MJjEN14uk

Figure 37. Artverau. (2014). Broccoli plant green. [photograph]. *Pixabay.*

https://pixabay.com/photos/broccoli-plant-green-food-organic-494753/

Figure 38. Pasti. (2017). Broccoli romanesco vegetable. [photograph]. *Pixabay.*

https://pixabay.com/photos/broccoli-romanesco-vegetable-2080830/

Figure 39. Tgd990. (2015). Purple broccoli small. [photograph]. *Pixabay.*

https://pixabay.com/photos/purple-broccoli-small-fresh-711208/

Figure 40. Congerdesign. (2015). Watermelon melon juicy. [photograph]. *Pixabay.*

https://pixabay.com/photos/watermelon-melon-juicy-fruit-food-815072/

Figure 41. Luong N. (2020).Cantaloupe grown on trellis. [photograph]. *Unsplash.*

https://unsplash.com/photos/lxQgjtg-es0

Figure 42. Suthriwala S. (2021). Sliced green fruit on white surface. [photograph]. *Unsplash.*

https://unsplash.com/photos/CDfi2gZSUv8

Figure 43. Shaked R. (2019). Green vegetable photo. [photograph]. *Unsplash.*

https://unsplash.com/photos/Eds_XGgQ9Tg

Figure 44. Tankilevitch P. (2019). Green plant in close up photography. [photograph]. *Pexels.*

https://www.pexels.com/photo/food-salad-healthy-garden-4519008/

Figure 45. Kozik a. (2021). Free stock photo of america food, breakfast, berries. [photograph]. *Pexels.*

https://www.pexels.com/photo/food-healthy-cabbage-vegetarian-6630123/

Figure 46. Taylor A. (2017). Sprout vegetable food. [photograph]. *Pixabay.*

https://pixabay.com/photos/sprouts-vegetable-food-healthy-2582679/

Figure 47. Foodism360. (2019). Kalettes pattern. I simply love Kalettes for their gorgeous colours and their sweet, nutty flavour. They are hybrids, a cross-breed between Brussels sprout and kale. Try them raw, delicious. [photograph]. *Unsplash.*

https://unsplash.com/photos/wQg0_LEKTUw

Figure 48. Verbruggen T. (2014). Cozy greenhouse. [photograph]. *Unsplash.*

https://unsplash.com/photos/cVYLIzF6Gh0

Figure 49. Foodism360. (2019). BORN 2B WILD. Wild spinach. Gotta love the magenta + green combination. [photograph]. *Unsplash.*

https://unsplash.com/photos/embNAQ6MHYA

Figure 50. Spiske M. (2016). Rearing tomatoes for self support. [photograph]. *Unsplash.*

https://unsplash.com/photos/vrbZVyX2k4I

Figure 51. Spratt A. (2019). Green leaf plants photo. [photograph]. *Unsplash.*

https://unsplash.com/photos/ubBBg-Usq6M

Figure 52. Kotsell A. Boxed raised vegetable garden on pallet collars with fitted glass greenhouse on top. Mustad red oriental salad, tomato plants and carrots are seen in the first greenhouse. In a Swedish garden. [photograph]. *Shutterstock.*

https://www.shutterstock.com/image-photo/boxed-raised-vegetable-garden-on-pallet-1758435260

Figure 53. No-longer-here. (2013). Spinach frozen. [photograph]. *Pixabay.*

https://pixabay.com/photos/spinach-frozen-spinach-frozen-163955/

Figure 54. MacInnes D. (2017). Frozen blueberries. [photograph]. *Unsplash.*

https://unsplash.com/photos/AWzlLLuD0xA

Figure 55. P. A. women's hands put cucumbers in a can for canning, home canning of vegetables. [photograph]. Shutterstock.

https://www.shutterstock.com/image-photo/womens-hands-put-cucumbers-can-canning-1237907080

Figure 56. Jackson D. (2021). Brown glass jars on white wooden shelf. [photograph]. *Pexels.*

https://www.pexels.com/photo/food-wood-vintage-farm-6611594/

Figure 57. Jimenez G. (2017). Poor mans garden. [photograph]. *Unsplash.*

https://unsplash.com/photos/jin4W1HqgL4

Figure 58. Elijas E. (2017). Red and green fruits on brown wooden bench. [photograph]. *Pexels.*

https://www.pexels.com/photo/red-and-green-fruits-on-brown-wooden-bench-5503338/

Figure 59. Herbert. (2019). Garden compost nature. [photograph]. *Pixabay.*

https://pixabay.com/photos/garden-compost-nature-bio-ground-4725522/

Figure 60. Zimmer M. A. (2014). Garden waste. [photograph]. *Pixabay.*

https://pixabay.com/photos/compost-garden-waste-bio-nature-419261/

Figure 61. MelGreenFR. (2021). Ecology waste. [photography]. *Pixabay.*

https://pixabay.com/photos/compost-ecology-waste-garden-6053136/

Figure 62. Monthira. Coffee ground, Coffee residue is applied to the tree and is a natural fertilizer, Gardening hobby. [photograph]. *Shutterstock.*

https://www.shutterstock.com/image-photo/coffee-ground-residue-applied-tree-natural-1023534823

Figure 63. M. W. (2017). Wheelbarrow farm crap. [photograph]. *Pixabay.*

https://pixabay.com/photos/wheelbarrow-farm-crap-agriculture-2188081/

Figure 64. Spiske M. (2018). Person fruit on grass photo. [photograph]. *Unsplash.*

https://unsplash.com/photos/fDvokTkwEZ8

Figure 65. Fotios L. (2018). Person digging on soil using garden shovel. [photograph]. *Pexels.*

https://www.pexels.com/photo/person-digging-on-soil-using-garden-shovel-1301856/

Figure 66. Rankin C. (2020). Rhubarb in a local farm raised garden. [photograph]. *Unsplash.*

https://unsplash.com/photos/tGUZpfDvB1s/info

Figure 67. AHatmaker. Wooden vegetable bed box with soil in the home garden. Ecology and homegrowing concept. [photograph]. *Shutterstock.*

https://www.shutterstock.com/image-photo/wooden-vegetable-bed-box-soil-home-1770020030

CPSIA information can be obtained
at www.ICGtesting.com
Printed in the USA
BVHW022021041121
620782BV00004B/228